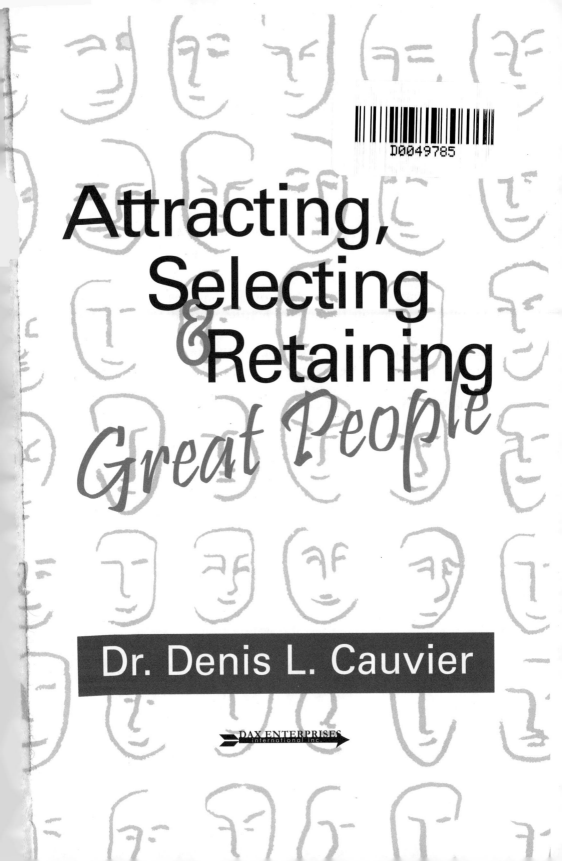

Attracting, Selecting & Retaining
Great People

Dr. Denis L. Cauvier

DAX ENTERPRISES
international inc.

Other Books by Dr. Denis L. Cauvier:

How to Hire the Right Person

How To Keep Your Staff Productive & Happy

Achieve It! A Personal Success Journal

The ABCs of Making Money (Co-authored by Alan Lysaght)

This publication is designed to provide competent and reliable information regarding the subject matter covered. However, it is sold with the understanding that the author and publisher are not engaged in rendering legal, financial, or other professional advice. Laws and practices often vary from country to country and state to state and if legal or other expert assistance is required, the services of a professional should be sought. The author and the publisher specifically disclaim any liability that is incurred from the use or application of the contents of this book.

First Edition, First Printing - Copyright © 2004 by DAX Enterprises International Inc.

ISBN 0-9736514-0-7

Publication design and layout by Donna Harris Design
Printed in Canada by Tri-Graphic Printing (Ottawa) Limited
10 9 8 7 6 5 4 3 2 1

Dedication

As always, to the three women in my life:

Sam – my first daughter who dances to the beat
of her own drum

Stevie – my second daughter who finds
laughter and delight in everything she does

and above all,

Debbie, my life partner

Acknowledgements

You can search the early evening sky a long time and find only one or two stars. After a long wait, another appears, then the next, and then a few more. Those you first squint at to keep in sight are finally joined by a myriad of stars that seem to appear all at once. And so it has been with writing this book. I'm grateful for the many who show their support now, but I am especially appreciative of those few stars who shone through the early stages of this project. To begin, I must thank my best friend and wife Debbie. She constantly supported me in the writing of this book by allowing me the time and space to think and create.

Secondly, I am also grateful for the design and layout work of Donna Harris. Donna, you especially went beyond the call of duty. To Lillian Cauvier for all of her help proofreading the manuscript, thanks mom! To my business partner Alan Lysaght for all the support. To Pat Norwood and the professional team at Tri-Graphic Printing (Ottawa) Limited for making the end product look so good.

Lastly, I wish to acknowledge the hundreds of thousands of people who have attended my seminars. I have learned and grown so much as a direct result of your feedback

A Personal Note from

Dr. Denis L. Cauvier

This book was written to help today's leaders deal more effectively, right now, with their number one issue—the "people" side of their businesses. In North America businesses are experiencing a growing concern for the level of productivity of their teams. Statistics have shown that not only is productivity slowly decreasing, but the available qualified work force is shrinking as well. No longer can leaders feel that, when a good person leaves the company, they'll "easily find someone else just as good." Now, more than ever, organizations feel the need to hang on to their current productive performers.

The average small- to -medium sized business in North America has had very little training or assistance in the area of attracting, selecting, leading, developing, and retaining great people. My first book, *How To Hire The Right Person* dealt specifically with the issues of attracting and selecting great people. My second, book *How To Keep Your Staff Productive And Happy* focused on the latter issues. This book takes the best principles covered in the first two books and is packaged in a "quick read" format designed specifically for today's busy leaders.

Attracting, Selecting & Retaining Great People, is the product of over 18 years experience as a professional speaker/trainer and consultant. Although the bulk of this book deals with lessons learned through direct experience, a great deal of what I know today was gleaned from a fairly relentless program of self-education, leading countless seminars, and workshops. This book draws together the best of the ideas I have been exposed to over the years. Although I have made considerable effort to indicate the source of any words that are not mine, I may have inadvertently failed to acknowledge the original source. If this has occurred I would be pleased to receive any information regarding the proper identification of sources.

Once you have the knowledge of the basics, the odds are in your favor. I sincerely hope you will be inspired to use this book as a constant source of practical information to ensure that you attract, select & retain great people.

Best wishes,

Dr. Denis L. Cauvier

Introduction

In my estimation the single biggest flaw in how corporate America conducts the typical recruiting assignment, is the over-emphasis placed on traditional criteria such as: the applicant's formal education, SAT scores, previous experience, and employment test results. Yes, these issues are relevant; they do reflect part of what the applicant has to offer. However, there are several other critical elements to consider when attracting & selecting great people. It is a shame that during the selection process these elements are often downplayed in their significance or outright overlooked. So what constitutes a great person? From a recruiting perspective I have developed the following way to view GREAT people.

- *G*oal oriented with a burning desire to win.
- *R*eputable with high moral standards and integrity.
- *E*nthusiastic about self-development.
- *A*ttitude of positive professionalism.
- *T*enacity to "do it" until the job gets done.

The challenge is that no accurate test exists to correctly assess how GREAT a person is, so most organizations don't bother investing much energy into this part of the process. By default they focus virtually all of their efforts on the more traditional elements. Conventional thinking has it that a candidate with an MBA, 20 years experience and an IQ of 162 should immediately be offered the job. I would argue that it's not that straight forward, that if this same person had a history of blaming others for their shortcomings, maintaining a negative attitude and possessing little ambition, they would likely be a poor performer. Contrast that individual with someone of average credentials and abilities, but who is coachable and has a burning desire to win, I will go out of my way to try to entice them to my team!

I believe that we need to examine all elements of the applicant, both their credentials and their character in order to make the wisest choice. This book will offer you insights on how to do both.

Overview of Attracting, Selecting & Retaining Great People

Seven Step Process

Table of Contents

The seven stages of Attracting, Selecting & Retaining Great People and the corresponding chapters outlined in the chart on the previous page are, in my opinion, absolutes. If you want to maximize your ability to attract, select & retain great people, I believe you must go through each and every one of these seven steps. If you take the time to read through them, you'll quickly come to the conclusion that these are all meaningful, worthwhile activities to engage in.

However, what typically happens is that it's often difficult to implement changes into your organization. Change involves coming out of one's "comfort zone" and going the extra mile. The fact is that we are all very busy people and, frankly, who has the time? My quick response to "who has the time to improve their attracting, selecting & retaining practices" is this brief story.

It was a hot July day in the town of Banff, Alberta. Two friends, a German and an American businessman, had decided to leave the conference they were attending and catch a breath of fresh air. They had walked several miles into the national park and were enjoying the beauty of the area when they decided to sit down and take off their shoes and socks so they would be able to feel the gentle pine needles under their feet. They got several yards down the path, when they heard a deep, loud growl coming from behind them. As soon as they heard the noise they turned around and came face to face with a grizzly bear. The German businessman decided to high-tail it down the path as fast as he could. After he ran about 100 yards, he turned around to see what was going on. He couldn't believe what he saw!

There was the American businessman calmly sitting at the edge of a large boulder putting on his socks and shoes, while the grizzly circled around him. Upon seeing this, the German businessman shouted, "The only way to outrun the bear is to get a head start." The American businessman replied, "The way I see it, I only have to outrun you!"

The moral of this story is that the American businessman understood one key principle of business: in order to be successful you have to take the time to be prepared before you enjoy the benefits of success. The parallel of this story to the attraction, selection & retention process is: once you take the time to identify your ideal recruit, select the best method of recruiting, and create the right corporate culture to assist your new person to develop their potential. With the suggestions and formats outlined in this book, you'll be better off than those leaders who constantly resist personal growth and change. The purpose of this book is to assist you in getting started, or to improve your ability to attract, select & retain great people. I will show you how to invest your time, energy and money wisely, so that your organization can reap the highest possible rewards for your efforts. If you follow the instructions and suggestions herein, you can avoid many of the common pitfalls. You took the first step when you purchased this book. The next step is to read it carefully and apply the advice. Take your time and proceed step-by-step. If you try to take shortcuts, you'll be increasing the odds of making costly errors.

Chapter ONE

You Can't Hit a Target You Can't See

*R*ecruiting a new person is not always the best answer. Perhaps you have enough people but the organization would be better served if the team was better trained, more efficient or better resourced. Prior to starting the recruiting process you may be well advised to determine the feasibility of recruiting an additional person. Therefore the critical question to ask is, do you really need to recruit at this time?

To determine this, consider the following questions:

Question 1:   What is the purpose of this new position?

Question 2:   Who is presently performing these tasks?

Question 3:   How long has the person who presently performs these tasks been overloaded?

Question 4:   Is this increase in business the result of a cycle or is the pace more permanent?

Question 5:   What will be the initial goals of this position, and how long will it take to accomplish them?

Question 6:   What are the best results we can expect if we fill this position?

Question 7:   Is there enough work for a full-time position, or can it be handled by a part-time person?

Question 8: Can some of the overload duties be transferred to another department or location?

Question 9: Is this a true need, or can this function be streamlined for better productivity?

Question 10: How much will this new position cost?

Question 11: Is there a significant labor market to choose from?

Question 12: Have you checked to determine if everyone affected feels there is a definite need?

Question 13: What is the worst that can happen if you don't create this position?

Once you've answered these questions to your satisfaction and have determined that a real need for recruitment exists, then proceed by completing a Job Description. Whenever I give a seminar or workshop on the uses of job descriptions, I normally kick it off with the following example. I'll ask my audience for a show of hands by asking how many people have ever shot a bow and arrow. Numerous people will raise their hands. I'll choose one person from the audience to come up on stage to help me illustrate my point. Once the volunteer is on stage, I ask them to imagine that there is a target set up at the back of the room, and on the table in front of them is a bow and arrow set. Once they can picture this, I ask them to act out the part of an archery instructor, with the audience as their class.

I have the volunteer describe, step-by-step, how to shoot an arrow. When they've gone through the cycle of positioning their body, holding the bow and arrow, aiming the arrow, pulling back the arm, lining up the target, breathing, and firing, I quickly recount the number of steps the "instructor" has just demonstrated. Although the steps may vary from as low as six to as high as twenty-one, the basic formula for success in hitting the target remains the same.

I now have my "instructor" stand in the readied position, and as I come behind him/her, I tell the audience that just prior to shooting the arrow I'm going to make two small changes. The first thing I do is place a black cloth bag over the head of the "instructor". The material of this bag is so heavy and dark it's impossible to see through it. I then take the "instructor" by the shoulders and gently spin the person around until they lose their orientation. When they're sufficiently disoriented, I tell them, without the aid of the audience or taking off the hood, they're to fire one imaginary arrow and hit the target the first time. Usually, the "instructor" makes a comment like, "What you're asking me to do is impossible." At that point I take off the hood, thank the volunteer, ask him/her to return to their seat, and ask the audience to give them a reward of applause.

By now, the confusion on the faces of my audience is evident. They have no idea what the point is. It is simply this: You can't hit a target you can't see! As in archery, if you lose sight or focus of your target, the likelihood of hitting your target is purely coincidental. Likewise in recruiting, you can go through all the steps and stages of attracting, interviewing, testing, etc., but if you haven't taken the time to determine what your target is, it's not likely that you're going to even hit it, let alone recognize it.

The power of the job description is that, as a tool, it helps us focus on our target: What key skills, knowledge and attitudes must the successful candidate possess for us to consider hiring them? When people don't take the time to identify their target, by having a quality job description prepared for the position, they often fall into a trap. Upon meeting an applicant that meets their basic criteria, they close their ears and turn their mouth on "auto sell." They close their mind to the screening process and focus all their energies on selling the position to this wonderful applicant, rather than examining the pros and cons from both sides.

Job descriptions are neither difficult nor time consuming to prepare if you tackle the issue the right way. I have included a blank job description you can use for your own needs. I will describe the significance of several areas I've identified in the sample.

JOB DESCRIPTION

Job Title: _____ Location: _____ Department:_____

Date Last Reviewed: _____ Title of Supervisor: _____

Job Summary: Briefly describe the purpose of this job, what is done and how.

_____

_____

Results: Describe the expected results.

_____

_____

What is the most difficult/demanding part of this job?

_____

_____

The qualifications and/or training that is required for this job are:

_____

_____

Now, divide the position into three key areas of responsibility. The responsibility could be further divided into three to five principal duties/tasks. List the knowledge and skills required for each duty.

1. Responsibility _____ Approximate % of time:_____

Duties/ Tasks:	Skills/ Knowledge Required	Priority

2. Responsibility _____ Approximate % of time:_____

Duties/ Tasks:	Skills/ Knowledge Required	Priority

3. Responsibility _____ Approximate % of time:_____

Duties/ Tasks:	Skills/ Knowledge Required	Priority

Character Profile

The ideal candidate will possess the following G.R.E.A.T characteristics:

Components of the Job Description

Date Last Reviewed:

This is important because it signifies how current the job description is. The rate of information in the world is doubling every 18 months. With rapid change all around us, it's bound to have an impact on the industries and companies we belong to, and a large impact on the positions within each company. I suggest that each job description be reviewed annually. In the event of a rapidly changing industry, I recommend as often as six months. Under extraordinary circumstances, i.e. a company merger or buy-out, these reviews and revisions should take place immediately following the change.

Job Summary

The job summary is a concise synopsis of a particular position. It tells what the job is, how it's done, and why. Within the summary, the responsibilities and job duties describe the specific tasks of the position. Each job can be broken down into several key responsibilities. Each responsibility can be further broken down into several duties. The job duties section is the most extensive component of the job description. The duties should be listed in descending order, beginning with the duty that most impacts the success of the job.

Results:

It is critical that both parties clearly understand the expected results of the position and how performance will be measured.

What Is The Most Difficult/Demanding Part of This Job?

By determining the most difficult or demanding aspects of the job, the leader can quickly identify potential stumbling blocks or pitfalls the employee will have to overcome in order to succeed. Knowing this helps the leader seek out individuals who either currently have strengths in this area, or become targeted areas for future training and development.

The Qualifications and/or Training Required for this Job:

It's very important, when identifying the skills required, that you do not limit your options from a potential pool of qualified applicants by requiring previous experience that could easily be replaced by training.

Prioritizing:

A method I've found successful in categorizing skills and abilities is the A.B.C. Formula: prioritize each duty, knowledge and skill by designating it as Absolute, Beneficial or Convenient to the success of the job.

Up to this point, the job description has focused on the "credentials" portion of the position. Unfortunately, most organizations stop the process here. The last section of the job description, The Character Profile targets the personal attributes of the ideal candidate. In my opinion, the "character" of the ideal person must be identified in advance in order to have a meaningful job description. Remember the lesson from archery, you can't hit a target you can't see!

Once all the components of the job description have been compiled, you will be able to correctly identify what a GREAT person means to your organization. Now you're ready to take the next step, covered in chapter two, the recruiting of great people.

Broadcasting the Message: Attracting Great People

*R*ecruitment is the process of finding and attracting great people that have both the right credentials and personal characteristics so that they will want to apply for the opportunity with your organization.

Successful recruiting stems largely from how a company makes the labor market aware of its employment opportunities. The recruiting program is only as effective as it's ability to hire great people.

There's no one best recruiting technique. Recruitment depends on the situation. The approach is influenced by job requirements, organizational and environmental constraints.

Finding great people is a continuing challenge for most companies. It's desirable for the recruiter to plan well in advance. Proper recruitment and selection takes time. In many cases, it means the difference between getting great people, and accepting inferior applicants.

There are two major types of recruiting methods: the search for suitable candidates from within the organization, and the search for candidates outside the organization.

The most progressive organizations have a policy whereby the initial attempt is made to fill positions from within. Besides reducing costs associated with external recruiting efforts, such "promote from within" policies serve to: boost team morale;

attract recruits looking for jobs with advancement opportunities (which, in turn, helps the company retain its present people); and reduce training costs, since the person is already oriented to the organization.

Below is an overview of the most common sources of recruitment.

Source	Pros	Cons
Own Staff	Individual is known	Limited choice
	Supports promote from within policy	No "new blood" from outside of the company
	Person has company knowledge	
Former Staff	Individual is known	Limited choice
	Low cost of recruiting	Potential challenges with former colleagues
	Person has company knowledge	
Employee Referrals	Low cost	Embarrassment if rejected
	Applicant has realistic expectation of job & company	Limited choice
		May be seen as "old boys club"
Private Employment Centers	Professional fees could cost less than actual internal costs requirements	Outdated lists of candidates
		Possible poor fit to job
	Dedicated full time HR professional	May not understand client's specific needs
Executive Search Firms	Dedicated full time HR professional	Sometimes they pursue avenues considered "unacceptable" by some company's standards
	Access to huge network	

Newspaper	Wide choice of applicants	Overwhelming number of applicants
		Shot-gun approach lacks focus
Educational Institutions	Minimum standards of knowledge of graduates	Often little previous relevant work experience
Professional Associations	Good for hard to find highly skilled people	Limited to size of association
Military Personnel	Extensively pre-trained, highly skilled, disciplined people	Only have access to people who have left or in process of leaving the military
Walk-ins	Available for work	Many will not be suitable
	Wants to work for your company	

Using the Net to Catch Great People

Looking for great people is much easier if you have the right tools. With global competition forcing companies to speed up their recruitment process what better tool to turn to than the computer, more specifically—the internet. Internet recruitment, often referred to as on-line recruitment, is a reality and quickly becoming the most cost-effective alternative to print and other media advertising when it comes to recruiting.

Back in 2000, over 8 million resumes were sent on-line to recruiters. That's up from 500,000 in 1996. Today, over 40 million prospective jobseekers have turned to the net to try to find that perfect job. By late 2005, it is predicted that 95 per cent of all companies with more than 50 people will integrate some form of on-line recruiting into their overall recruitment strategy. Like the fisherman who ditched the rod at the side of the riverbank for the factory freezer trawler and fishing nets, leaders need to shed the traditional mindset of recruiting and embrace the advantages of IT in recruiting. Learning how to tap into the power of the technology, and how to design e-recruitment ad copy is a new job skill for leaders. The traditional recruiting process requires time to sift through applications, pre-screen candidates, then start the preliminary interview process. On-line also saves time and money by pre-qualifying and pre-screening candidates before interviews are even scheduled.

More and more companies are realizing the benefits of recruiting on-line. With the increased jobseeker's access through home-based networks, universities, trade schools and related industry networks throughout the world, on-line has instant reach to the global society. No longer is recruitment limited by geographical constraints. Available 24 hours, 7 days a week, the possibilities are endless. Standardized resumes and job applications can be received in a format designed by the leader to meet the organization's needs.

On-line recruiting enables prospective recruits to surf the net for the right job that fulfills their needs. Not only can they mass distribute resumes and CVs, but through company web sites or interactive recruitment networks they can find out about a company's structure, job descriptions, information and/or links to relevant industry and job related sites.

The following are URLs of some of the largest and better known on-line recruitment portals.

- www.monster.com
- www.careers.yahoo.com
- www.hotjobs.com
- www.jobshark.com
- www.workopolis.com

For the recruiter, choosing the right on-line recruitment provider is crucial to your success. The following questions can be used as a guide in selecting the right on-line portal to meet your recruitment needs:

- How recruiter-friendly and applicant-friendly is the e-recruitment service?

- Is the traffic (local or international) on the site targeted to your recruiting needs?
- Does the database offer quality as well as quantity?
- Are the ads timely and editable?
- Does the service offer links to other relevant web sites, provide on-line management of short-listed prospects, and secure data transmission?
- Does the site provide a "live" person for tech support?

Sound intimidating? It need not be. On-line recruiting is not the destination, however, but a tool in the journey with the final goal being to recruit great people in the most time and cost effective manner. Those who understand the potential of e-recruitment will capitalize on it. Like the fisherman, the quality of his net will help him reel-in the best catch.

Independent Contractors

An alternative to hiring someone is to engage the services of an independent contractor. There are a lot of advantages to this: the person works only when you need them, you don't have to provide benefit packages, lay someone off, or deal with all the accompanying paperwork. One of the cautions to this method is that you can contract your business away.

A good friend of mine, who has a large speaking and training business decided he didn't want the traditional headaches associated with standard employer/employee relationships. He felt his operation would be simplified by hiring independent trainers who had an existing client base. Unfortunately, what happened was that these people simply added his client base to theirs at the end of the contract, which cost him potential earnings in excess of $5 million and nearly put him out of business.

Opportunity Meetings

Many companies have used some form of "Opportunity Meeting" as a method of recruiting. This type of recruiting is generally used by Direct-Sales companies and Multi-Level Marketing Networks. Often they use these meetings to "hard-sell" people in attendance to purchase a lot of expensive products/ services and or pay a very high "business start-up fee," as opposed to being a true recruiting campaign. An example of a company that has taken a very different approach to opportunity meetings are those conducted by Primerica Financial Services Limited. The fundamental difference is that their recruiting is largely based on educating attendees on how to become debt-free and financially independent while providing them with the opportunity to make money educating others. This type of recruiting provides an excellent opportunity for people who perhaps had not previously considered this type of career, to learn more about what a company has to offer and draw their own conclusions.

Volunteer Associations

One of the best places to find someone with leadership skills is through a volunteer association. For instance, the person that's going to head up the telemarketing fund-raising campaign for the American Heart Foundation will be accountable for many things, e.g. organizing and co-coordinating the campaign, and revving up dozens of volunteers to achieve the campaign goals. This person usually possesses excellent interpersonal and motivational skills, and natural leadership qualities.

One of the challenges of leading a group of volunteers is that these people work very hard without drawing a pay check, so you can't motivate them by financial incentive or from the fear of getting fired. Nevertheless, an effective fund-raising captain will lead their team through numerous obstacles, while achieving a high rate of success.

Competitors

In the summer of 1982, I was the manager of a pizza franchise, and I was having what can be categorized as a crummy day. Within a two-hour span, two waitresses and one waiter gave notice (each for personal reasons) that they were leaving by the end of the week. Faced with this dilemma, I did what any good leader would do—I went to the local burger restaurant. I placed myself in a strategic location so I could overlook the activity at the front counter.

What I saw was a young woman, named Leslie, who was out-performing the other six workers on the line. Leslie had the ability to up-sell more fries, drinks and desserts than half the other staff. While her counterparts droned on in an automated voice, "Will there be anything else?" Leslie was busy up-selling her clients in a friendly, natural manner. After watching her in action for about a half hour, including the way she dealt with a sexual advance from an intoxicated customer, I was convinced she possessed the necessary attributes to be a successful waitress at my restaurant.

I approached Leslie, introduced myself, and asked her how much money she made per hour. She said she made minimum wage. I asked her if she'd be interested in working for double that amount, guaranteed. Upon hearing this, her eyes enlarged substantially, she leaned over and gasped, "Is this legal?" I replied that not only was it legal, but it could also provide a job that was more enjoyable than the one she was currently doing.

I explained my position, my predicament, and the opportunity I was offering her. She asked me how she could capitalize on my job offer. I said, "Grab your coat, leap over this counter, and let's get to work!" I was shocked by her reply, "I'm sorry, Mr. Cauvier, I won't be able to take you up on your offer unless I could give my employer two weeks notice." Hearing this, I was prepared to present her with the ultimatum, "Take my offer now, or never." I decided against such a quick reaction, because I felt that if she was going to pay the courtesy of giving her employer notice, she would probably never leave me in a bind. This was a great illustration of someone with the right attitude.

We agreed she would start working for me two weeks from that date. Asking if there was anything else she could do for me, I replied, "Is there anyone else here that I should be looking at?" She suggested I look at the young lady at the take-out window, and survey the cooking area. I said, "You can't be serious—not the burger flipper!" To this, she said, "Take several moments and just watch these people, I think you'll be impressed." Well, impressed I was; the young woman at the take-out window had a tremendous way of dealing with the customers and was very efficient, and the cook at the back was a true leader. He encouraged team support and maintained the pace of the entire kitchen. His people skills were substantially greater than his years would suggest. I hired the three of them.

Four years later, when I had the opportunity to visit that pizza restaurant, I learned that the two women servers were leaders in inside sales, and the young man had moved on to a senior management position within the company.

The point is that we sometimes look for people with specific experience, i.e. must have previous experience as a waiter/waitress. If I had held fast to that criteria I would never have considered the last two people. Really, what was needed was to find three individuals with superior people skills and a track record of being client-driven.

I'm not suggesting that you steal from your competitors, but I am saying don't be rigid in your search for suitable staff.

Community Religious Leaders

Your local clergy are well connected and informed about their congregants who are seeking employment. Also, these people can provide a personal viewpoint as to the character of the individual.

Physically and Mentally Challenged Individuals

Properly placed, workers with disabilities have greater stability and less turnover than non-disabled workers. Seventy percent of workers with disabilities have attendance records equal to or better than those of non-disabled workers. More and more people with disabilities are attaining higher education and training, and qualifying for responsible, career-track positions. Legislation coupled with increasing social awareness, is opening doors for disabled persons to demonstrate their abilities in the workplace. "Employment equity goes beyond responding to government or special interest groups; it is not about quotas, sympathy or tokenism. Employment Equity is about hiring and promoting good people from previously under-utilized sources. It's good business sense," says Bob Sutherland, Senior Vice President and General Manager, Atlantic Provinces, Royal Bank of Canada.

Seniors and Semi-Retirees

A recent trend is to look at retired individuals as a source of knowledge and experience to bring into your organization either on a contract or employee basis. Many mature adults have a lot to give, and are dissatisfied with the lifestyle associated with being retired.

Numerous agencies have sprouted up to help match seniors with employers. Examples of these are Seniors for Hire, Grey-Power and Seniors for Business.

Minorities and Aboriginals

Numerous minorities and aboriginals are taking advantage of the increased educational programs and incentives offered by government. This previously under-utilized group are now competing for all types of occupations, and effectively integrating into the employment mainstream.

Women Re-Entering the Workforce

Although women who are re-entering the workforce may have business or other skills that are somewhat outdated, they still possess a wealth of positive attributes. They're mature, responsible, effective time and stress managers, problem solvers, and have the ability to organize and juggle many tasks at a time. With a bit of technology up-grading and/or training, these women can be one of your greatest assets.

For referrals, contact your local YWCA, or the Displaced Homemakers Network at area code 202-628-6767. In Canada there are various Employment Outreach Programs located in most major centers, and the Canadian Advisory Council on the Status of Women at 613-992-4975.

Moonlighters

In the past, many employers haven't looked very favorably upon moonlighters, but as times change and we require individuals that are more flexible, this particular pool of recruits can be advantageous because of their flexibility. Some classic examples of this are teachers, police officers, firefighters, seasonally employed workers, retail clerks, nurses, off-shore oil riggers, fishermen, coast guards, flight attendants, railway workers, and the like. Shift workers are often talented individuals who want to supplement their regular income by working part-time.

Reminder: Don't limit your thinking to one sex or the other. For instance, there are a lot of male nurses and secretaries coming into the picture, as well as female pilots, astronauts and steeplejacks. In other words, make your recruiting non-gender based.

Recruiting is Broadcasting

Recruitment is a marketing function, since it's really a process of selling the opportunity to prospective recruits. Recruiters need to be honest about what the opportunity entails and must avoid overselling candidates on the company, since this can lead to disillusionment, resulting in staff turnover. Over-selling the company can result in an accusation of false advertising, and can do extensive damage to the firm's reputation, which could adversely affect future recruitment. Recruitment activity should, therefore, be creative, imaginative, honest and innovative.

For example, proper word choice in recruiting materials is essential. Words such as rapidly expanding, nationally known, or leading, to describe the company, do more to attract potential recruits than words like "old" or "big". The style of recruiting material should be simple and direct, answering the applicant's primary question: "What's in it for me?" It's advisable to personalize the material through the use of such pronouns as "you" and "your."

The recruiter must ask a fundamental question: "What are the objectives of the recruitment material?" Typically, there are five main objectives for recruitment material:

- to eliminate those people who are not appropriate for the opportunity

- to attract suitable candidates for the job

- to motivate as many appropriate people as possible to apply

- to reach the best people as economically as possible

- to enhance the overall reputation of the company by the image projected in the recruitment material

No single recruitment technique is effective at all times, under all circumstances, and for all companies. Most companies have found they must be prepared to quickly adapt their methods to the constantly changing nature of the labor market.

Post-Recruitment

The recruitment process ends when an applicant formally applies for the opportunity, usually by completing an application form or submitting their resume. This does not mean, however, that the work of the recruiter is completed at this point. The recruiter should obtain feedback from interviewers and leaders in charge of selection, to ensure that current recruitment efforts are bringing in great people.

Chapter THREE

Prescreening, Finding The Best People In The Crowd

*Y*ou've taken the time to attract a large pool of people and you only have one position to fill. Are you going to interview all ninety-two secretaries? I would hope not! What you need to do is reduce the size of this group to only three to five interviewees. The best ways to quickly screen out applicants who don't match your requirements are: a) evaluate their resumes and covering letters, b) study their application forms, c) check references.

Pre-interview screening provides an efficient means to determine if the applicant has the credentials, in other words, "can they do the job?" The interviewing stage, discussed in the next chapter, is concerned with exploring the candidate's character, that is to say, "is he or she the best person for this job?"

One creative way to save yourself time and energy in prescreening is to invite interested applicants to personally drop off their resume and covering letter. This method works well for weeding out those who may have difficulty finding your offices, or discovering it could be too far for them to commute to work, too expensive for weekly parking, or there's something about the location of your workplace they don't like.

For those who come to your office, I suggest you provide them with a job description for the position they're applying for. After reading it, they may realize that the job is not suited for them, and opt to discontinue their application. Look at the time, energy and money you can save if a large number of your applicants screen themselves out in this manner.

If the applicant wants to pursue the opportunity further, ask them to fill out your detailed application form. This is a quick indicator of their level of intent and interest in working for your company. You may also want to ask them to write a paragraph about themselves. This particular exercise isn't applicable for every position, but it will indicate a certain level of competency in writing skills and penmanship, should the position require such skills.

What Should Be Included in Your Application Form?

Your application form should be designed to provide the information you need to evaluate both the credentials and character of the applicant. Included on the next page is a sample job application form.

Job Application Form

We are an equal employment employer, we consider applicants for all positions without regard to race, color, religion, sex, national origin, age, marital status, the presence of a non-job-related medical condition or disability.

(The more you write, the easier it is for us to know if you are going to fit within our company. Attach extra paper as necessary.)

Position Applied For: _____ Date of Application: _____

How did you learn about us? _____

Applicant Information

Name: _____ Social Insurance Number: _____

Address:_____

City: _____ State/Province: _____ Zip/Postal Code: _____

Telephone: (home): _____ (email): _____

Are you legally permitted to work in this country?   ☐ Yes   ☐ No

Education and Training:

Circle the highest grade in years completed.

8 9 10 11 12 13	1 2 3 4	1 2 3 4
High School	Trade School	University

Please provide the following information about your education. (include high school, trade and vocational schools and universities:

School Name	Degree/Diploma	Address	Date Started	Date Completed

Special qualifications or certifications. (include name of institution, start and completion date of program, grade achieved.):_____

Industry/Business training. (include business and industry seminars and workshops.):

Course: _____ Date taken: _____

Company or institution providing training: _____

What did you learn? _____

Course: _____ Date taken: _____

Company or institution providing training: _____

What did you learn? _____

Employment History

Present employer: _____

Address: _____

Telephone: _____ Supervisor: _____

Type of business: _____

Job Title: _____

Job Duties: _____

Why are you leaving? _____

_____

What would your employer say about you? _____

_____

May we contact your present employer? ☐ Yes ☐ No

Past employers: (begin with the most recent)

Name of Business: _____

Address: _____

Telephone: _____ Supervisor: _____

Type of business: _____

Job Title: _____

Job Duties: _____

Why are you leaving? _____

_____

What would your employer say about you? _____

Name of Business: _____

Address: _____

Telephone: _____ Supervisor: _____

Type of business: _____

Job Title: _____

Job Duties: _____

Why are you leaving? _____

_____

What would your employer say about you? _____

_____

Name of Business: _____

Address: _____

Telephone: _____ Supervisor: _____

Type of business: _____

Job Title: _____

Job Duties: _____

Why are you leaving? _____

_____

What would your employer say about you?_____

_____

Personal History

What are your special interests and activities? _____

_____

What teams have you worked or played on? _____

To be an effective team player what must a person do or not do?

_____

_____

What special knowledge and skills do you bring to this job?

_____

_____

What are your personal strengths and weaknesses?

a. Strengths: _____

b. Weaknesses: _____

What are your personal and career goals?

a. Personal: _____

b. Career: _____

Why do you want this job?

_____

_____

Anything else you wish to tell us about yourself?

_____

_____

May we contact you at work?   ☐ Yes   ☐ No

If no, how do we reach you during the day?

_____

By my signature on this application, I:

a. Authorize the verification of the above information and any other necessary inquiries that may be necessary to determine my suitability for employment.

b. Affirm that the above information is true.

Applicant's Signature: _____ Date: _____

As you review the above sample, you may wonder why all this information is requested on the form, when it can be obtained during the interview. During the earlier stages of the selection process the majority of the screening out should happen with a minimum amount of your effort. Because your time is valuable, a detailed application form is an efficient tool that helps to streamline the screening process by using the applicant's time and energy to screen themselves out. Although it may take the applicant a half-hour to fill out the form, it should only take you several moments to read it. To obtain this caliber of information during the interview, it usually takes a fair amount of time.

As you may have noted the first three pages of the application blank focused on the person's credentials while the fourth page provides further insight into the applicant's character.

There are a number of potential danger signs one should be looking for when reviewing applications:

1. An erratic job history with several periods of unemployment or job-hopping.

2. Major gaps in employment that are unaccounted for.

3. Salary expectations that exceed what the position pays.

4. Frequent changes of residence.

5. Considerable detail regarding previous experience or education which is irrelevant to the position.

6. Reasons for leaving previous jobs that suggest there were some possible negative issues.

7. Health challenges or physical disabilities that would prevent the individual from performing the duties of that specific job.

Covering Letters and Resumes

There's an old saying in advertising: Let the Buyer Beware. The same holds true for recruiting. Remember that resumes provide you with a one-sided look at the applicant, the positive side. Resumes, by their very nature, help applicants put their best foot forward. Keep in mind that what is not said in the covering letter and resume is as important as what is said. The following is a guideline on what to look for when reviewing resumes to better determine if the applicant is a great person for this opportunity.

1. Does the applicant demonstrate a sense of achievement and accomplishment in their resume? Past performance is indicative of likely future performance. If the person has had a successful track record of being an achiever in the past, chances are that this trend will continue.

2. Is the applicant profit and cost conscious? Any candidate who brings to light how they can have a dramatic impact on increasing the profits or reducing the costs of operating the business is, in my estimation, someone who is worthy of having a closer look at. Sometimes, one of the difficulties we face is having staff who possess the skills and knowledge to physically do the job, but they don't look at their job in light of the whole organization, and don't really see how they have a profound impact on the overall financial well-being of the company.

3. Is the candidate client-driven? My friend, Bill Gibson, has a slogan he uses often: "everyone is in sales." It doesn't matter whether you're the president of the company, a janitor or a receptionist; everyone, at one point or another, has to progressively and effectively market the good name of the company.

4. Has the applicant demonstrated stability? Stability and dependability are two issues that are near and dear to most leaders' hearts. If you look at a resume and see that the applicant has a history of changing jobs that appears excessive, I would urge you to be somewhat cautious when considering this individual, because you may be just one more stepping stone for them. Yet, if someone has been able to change jobs frequently, there must be some good in this person because they've been able to repeatedly sell

themselves to various organizations. Look at the applicant, get a feel for what their goals are, compare them to what you're offering, and ask yourself, "Will this job satisfy this person, or will they be somewhat disillusioned and disappointed and continue their job-hopping venture?"

5. Is the applicant goal-oriented? When I'm reviewing resumes, I'm interested in the degree of personal and professional goals that the applicant has demonstrated. What I'm looking for is someone who has a burning desire to win.

6. Does the applicant possess a solid work ethic? Although it's difficult to determine the exact extent of their work ethic from the resume alone, you can certainly get clues. For instance, any time I've seen a person volunteer for numerous worthwhile endeavors, I interpret it as a sign of someone who's prepared to go that extra mile. Also, if their job performance exceeds the actual responsibilities for the positions held, it's another indicator of someone who's prepared to work that much harder. But be cautious, if you sense that the applicant's mind-set indicates, "Oh, I can't do that because it's not in my job description" and you notice an unwillingness to be flexible, I would suspect they're not the type of person you'd want.

7. How much information has the applicant disclosed in their resume? Has the applicant "beefed up" the personal section with a long list of various interests and hobbies? If so, this may indicate someone who'd rather play than work, or someone who doesn't have a lot of experience.

Another caution is when you see phrases in the resume like: "has experience at," "has knowledge of," "has assisted with," "is familiar with." These phrases are vague, and can often be an attempt to puff up one's skill-base more than is actually warranted. When I see this, then challenge the applicant, invariably I find they lack the hands-on experience that was suggested they have.

If a resume contains comments similar to: "I didn't really enjoy this," or "It was so-and-so's fault," these are classic examples of someone with a negative attitude. I would suggest you trash these applications immediately. Anyone who is that negative and bitter in their resume is likely not the kind of person any of us would want on our team.

Although a book with an attractive cover will warrant a second glance, it doesn't guarantee a sale. This is also true for resumes. Be on guard for "slick" resumes. Look beyond the surface appearance to the actual information it contains.

Once you've gone through all the resumes, the next step is to screen them. One of the quickest methods is to divide the pile into three smaller ones. These represent "yes," "maybe," and "no." Set up interviews with the "yes" applicants, send rejection letters to the "no" applicants, and place the "maybes" in a pending file to be used as a backup.

It is unfortunate that there are people who lie on their resumes. Some people claim to have university degrees that they never received. Others claim to have worked for companies that never employed them.

The best way to guard against such falsifications is to conduct a quality reference check.

Reference Checking

It is a little-known fact that ninety percent of all hiring mistakes can be prevented through proper reference-checking procedures. Unfortunately, the vast majority of recruiters do not take the time to do this. Instead, they rely on their own impressions or "gut" feeling of the candidate based on the covering letter, resume, application form and interview. This is a mistake. As I've mentioned before, hiring the wrong person can be very costly.

Checking references is absolutely essential. It's estimated that one-third of all job applicants lie on their resumes, covering letters or application forms, or exaggerate their accomplishments. This underscores the necessity to check references.

Why is it so many recruiters don't conduct quality reference checks?

The number one reason, in my estimation, is that they don't realize how important this is. The second reason is that many recruiters don't know how to go about it. The third reason is that this activity can be very time-consuming. In many cases, there's great pressure to hire someone quickly. Conducting improper reference checks has led to an increasing number of lawsuits against companies. This trend has caused organizations to become very cautious about giving out information regarding former employees. Some companies have policies that expressly prohibit the release of employee information other than name, title, and length of employment.

Many people ask me when a reference check should be conducted. It should take place prior to the interview. A lot of people conduct reference checks after the interview. In my opinion, this is a non-productive use of time. An effective reference check can be done in less than one-quarter of the time it takes to conduct an interview. Therefore, if the check is done first, an undesirable applicant can be screened out, and the interview time saved.

In addition, checking references before the interview enables the interviewer to formulate questions to be asked during the interview. It's a good practice to seek permission from the applicant before checking references. Contacting the current employer without prior written permission is against the law in many jurisdictions. Furthermore, many job applicants don't want their current employer to know they're seeking opportunities elsewhere. To deal with this particular challenge, let the applicant know that a written offer of employment will be contingent on receipt of a satisfactory reference from their current employer. (You reserve the right to withdraw the offer of employment if a satisfactory reference is not received.) By doing this, you will circumvent the challenge of not being able to contact the present employer. At the same time, you'll also encourage the applicant to be truthful with their responses, since both the prospective position and their present job could be put at risk by failing to tell the truth.

There are three different methods to check references: in person, by mail, and by telephone. Although checking references in person is the most reliable and effective means of obtaining information about the applicant, it's also the least practical. However, when possible, there are several advantages to face-to-face meetings with an applicant's former employer. In a personal meeting, you can discern the non-verbal reaction. You'll also find that, behind closed doors and without telephone disturbance, people will tend to be more candid.

Checking references by mail, or email is the least effective means of obtaining reference information, for three reasons:

1. This can be a tremendously slow process.

2. Many former employers are unlikely to respond due to the time involved in writing down their thoughts.

3. Many people hesitate to put anything in writing about past employees.

Telephone reference-checking is the most common and effective means of obtaining pertinent information about the applicant. One advantage of this method is that it's very time effective, and you can get immediate response or clarification. Although you, can't see the respondent, you miss out on seeing the body language, you can still pick up on subtle nuances in their voice. Look for signs of hesitation, tone of voice, and long-winded answers, particularly when you ask the critical question, "Would you rehire this person?"

Included is a sample telephone reference check form. Use it as a guide to conduct your next reference check. Any responses above or below average would warrant further investigation. This can be accomplished by asking, "Can you give me some examples of why you rated the applicant that way?"

Telephone Reference Check

Good day, my name is _____ of _____,
_____is being considered for
employment in the position of _____ . Your name has
been given as a former employer. We would greatly appreciate
your evaluation of this applicant's performance. The following
information has been given to us. Please verify.

Employed from: _____ to: _____   Yes ____   No____ Pay: _____
                                       Yes ____   No____

Position held: _____   Yes ____   No____

Please rate this applicant on the following items:

Criteria	Above Avg.	Average	Below Avg.	Comments
Performance, compared to others:				
Supervision and Guidance requirements				
Job related skills:				
Reaction to stress and change:				
Regularity of attendance:				
Meeting deadlines:				
Communications:				
Willingness to learn:				
Acceptance of direction from others:				
Acceptance of criticism from others:				
Ability to get along with others:				
Leadership qualities:				
Dependability:				
Positive attitude:				

Other: _____

Reason for termination: _____

Would you rehire? Yes ___ No ___

 If *No*, why not?_____

Raters Name: _____

Rater's Department: _____

Rater's Position: _____

Relation to applicant: _____

Company: _____

Location: _____

If you take your time, you'll find that the pre-screening stage of the recruiting process can save you a tremendous amount of time and energy. It will help you screen out applicants who didn't possess the credentials and character that you are looking for.

Chapter FOUR

Getting to Know Each Other

The principal reason for a selection interview is to determine which of the pre-screened candidates is the best person for the job. However there is, an additional purpose—for the interviewer to familiarize the applicant with the opportunities and the company.

A thought to keep foremost in your mind is that the interview is intended to narrow down the number of likely prospects for a position. As an interviewer, you're going to ask yourself these key questions: "How well will the applicant fit in with the company?" and "To what degree would the company benefit if the candidate was hired?"

Five Basic Interview Formats

Interviews are commonly conducted on a one-to-one basis between the interviewer and the candidate, however, group interviews are sometimes used. One form of group interview is to have the applicant meet with two or more interviewers. These people could be several department leaders, or peers that the recruit would be working with. This format allows each interviewer to evaluate the individual on the basis of the same questions and answers. Reliability is therefore improved.

Another variation is to have two or more applicants interviewed together by one or more interviewers. This saves time, especially for busy executives. It also permits the answers from different applicants to be compared immediately. The format will correspond to the position you're seeking to fill, as well as the interviewing procedures adopted by your company.

The internet provides a low cost alternative for the initial face-to-face interview especially when factoring the high cost of travel. Through web-based video conferencing both parties can be brought together in a virtual face-to-face contact.

The five formats of interviews are unstructured, structured, mixed, problem-solving and stress producing. The most appropriate of the formats depends on the position you're trying to staff, the philosophy of your company, and your style preference.

The *Unstructured Interview* allows for the development of questions as the interview progresses. The interviewer explores topic areas as they arise in conversation. Due to the lack of control with this approach, reliability suffers, since each applicant is asked a different set of questions. This can result in a waste of the interviewer's time, and the potential to overlook areas of an applicant's skills or background.

In the *Structured Interview*, questions are standard and predetermined. This allows the interviewer to cover specific areas, and identify the candidate's personal strengths and weaknesses. Specific answers regarding an applicant's qualifications and experience can be obtained with this approach, and improves the reliability of the interview process; but it doesn't allow the interviewer to follow up on interesting or unusual responses. One disadvantage to this method is that the interview may seem mechanical, and it may convey a lack of interest to candidates who are used to more flexible interviews.

The *Mixed Interview* is the most widely used interviewing technique. It's a combination of the unstructured and structured interviews. With this format, the interviewer follows a predetermined plan, but deviates from it to query important details.

Solutions Based Interviews focus on a challenge or series of issues that the candidate is expected to solve during the course of the interview. Both the answer and the approach taken by the applicant are evaluated. This format is limited in scope, yet it has one advantage: it reveals the applicant's ability to solve a variety of situational challenges. The actual interview might consist of ten scenarios. For example, the interviewer asks: "Suppose you notice the secretary make a copy of a computer software program, and then place the disk into her purse. What would you do?"

The *Stress-producing Interview* is effective when staffing positions that involve high levels of stress, such as a police officer. The purpose of this format is to put the applicant under pressure to determine how well he/she can cope. This technique catches the applicant off guard in order to gauge their response. This is accomplished by asking a series of harsh questions in rapid succession, and in a firm manner. In my opinion, since stress is usually only part of a job, this technique should only be used in conjunction with one of the other four interview formats.

Interview Phases

The structure of an interview can best be described in five phases. Each phase has its own purpose and is intended to accomplish certain goals. An awareness of the purpose of each phase and the goals you're trying to accomplish makes the entire process smooth and effective. The five phases that each interviewer goes through are: preparation, opening, exchange of information, closing and evaluation.

Preparation:

You must prepare yourself prior to the interview. Specific questions must be developed in advance. It's the answers to these questions that you will use in deciding the applicant's suitability. At the same time, some consideration should be given to what questions the applicant is likely to ask. Since the interview should also be used to prepare top applicants to accept subsequent job offers, you as the interviewer need to be able to explain job duties, performance standards, pay, benefits, and other areas of interest beyond the scope of the specific job opening.

The Opening:

During the opening, the interviewer and interviewee get acquainted, and the attempt is made to put the interviewee at ease. By taking the time to help the applicant relax, you will be reducing his/her level of stress. This will help the applicant converse more freely, and you'll receive answers that accurately reflect the true characteristics of the applicant. You can help this along by exchanging typical social amenities such as shaking hands, taking the applicant's coat, offering them a chair (and coffee if appropriate), introducing yourself, and beginning with some informal discussion. The interviewer should always explain the procedure that will be followed during the interview. This serves to put the candidate further at ease by letting them know what's generally going to happen and approximately how long it will take. The candidate will also be reassured that there will be an opportunity to ask questions towards the end of the interview.

Exchange of Information:

The body of the interview is the assessment period. Here, the interviewer fulfills the primary objective of gathering the information that will help determine whether the applicant fits the job. Obviously, the way the exchange of information is conducted is crucial. The interviewer needs to ask appropriate questions, solicit pertinent responses, and constantly evaluate the applicant's verbal and non-verbal expressions.

The Closing:

After you have solicited all the information you need to make the hiring choice, it's time to close the interview. Here, both the applicant and the interviewer have a chance to meet some of their objectives. The applicant has an opportunity to find out what they want to know about the position, the organization, and prospective co-workers. The interviewer, in addition to answering the applicant's queries, has the chance to further evaluate the applicant's values, and to sell the candidate on the company and the job, if appropriate.

Let the applicant know when you expect to make a decision and how he/she will be contacted. Being clear about the steps you intend to take will set the applicant at ease about the waiting period that follows the interview. Be careful not to say anything that could be misconstrued as a job offer.

Evaluation:

Immediately following the interview, the interviewer should record specific answers and general impressions. A post-interview report is a checklist used to record the interviewer's impressions.

Using a checklist, like the one that follows, can improve the reliability of the interview or selection technique.

What Are the Best Questions to Ask?

Since the crux of the interview is the exchange of information, your effectiveness as a interviewer is extremely important. For many people, asking critical questions can be the most difficult part of the interview. On the surface, questioning may appear to be a simple skill, however, effective questioning can take many years to master. It's unprofessional to initiate an interview without a strategy for obtaining the information you need. The position you're trying to fill will determine the kind of information you will want to collect. By reviewing the job description, you can familiarize yourself with the qualifications the position requires. It's advisable to follow a pre-planned progression of questioning. This will reduce the probability of confusing various applicants with one another. You may decide to restructure the progression of your questions. Variations are acceptable, as long as they allow the interview to proceed smoothly.

Open-Ended Questions:

Using open-ended questioning is an effective way to increase both the quantity and quality of information during an interview. An open-ended question is one that allows for an expanded range of responses. It allows you to glimpse how the applicant thinks, gauge the applicant's communication skills, and scrutinize the applicant's ability to organize his/her responses. Questions that begin with the words who, what, where, when, why and how, solicit open responses. Open-ended questions might also start with a phrase such as "Tell me…" An open-ended question is one that's impossible to answer with Yes or No. Also, it does not suggest to the applicant what specific kinds of information the interviewer wants. It does not suggest what the interviewer considers important, nor does it imply that a given answer will be considered correct.

By encouraging the candidate to answer in their own way, you place the responsibility for carrying the conversation on the applicant. The 70/30 rate of communications applies during the interviewing process, with the interviewer speaking no more than thirty percent of the time. By listening and observing the rest of the time, one can learn new things about the candidate.

When using this questioning technique, you may be asked by the candidate, "What exactly would you like to know?" Your response should be: "I don't have anything specific in mind. Feel free to say whatever you like."

When asking open-ended questions, be prepared for some silence on the part of the applicant. A few-second pause is normal. This allows the candidate to collect their thoughts to form an answer. You may need to rephrase questions or probe for more detail if you don't find out what you're after.

I have listed 101 sample open-ended questions that could be asked during the interview.

101 Great Interview Questions

Interviewee's Name: _____

Position Applied for: _____

Date: _____ Name Of Interviewer: _____

Work Experience

Cover: Earliest jobs, part time, temporary, full time positions.

Things to look for: Relevance of work

Sufficiency of work

Skill and competence

Adaptability

Productivity

Motivation

Interpersonal relations

Leadership

Growth and development

Ask:

1. Could you describe your career with _____?

2. Tell me about your work experience in general terms, beginning with your job as _____ and leading up to your present job.

3. Tell me about some of your achievements that have been recognized by your superiors.

4. Please describe your present duties and responsibilities.

5. Would you tell me more specifically about your duties with _____?

6. What do you feel were some of your most important accomplishments in your job as _____?

7. What are some of the reasons for considering other employment at this time?

8. How would you describe your present/past supervisor? What do you consider to have been his/her major strengths and weaknesses?

9. What are some things your supervisors have complimented you on? What have they criticized?

10. How do you think your present/past supervisor would describe you?

11. What are some of the things you particularly like about your job as_____?

12. What did you enjoy less?

13. What are some things that frustrate you most in your present job?

14. What were some of the setbacks and disappointments you experienced?

15. What were some problems you encountered on your job as _____ and how did you solve them?

16. What is your impression of _____?

17. Why did you leave ___ _____?

18. Why are you pursuing a career as a_____?

19. Tell me about your training. What have you done to improve yourself professionally?

20. What do you like least about the job description?

21. Tell me about a sale that was, for all intents and purposes, lost. How did you turn the situation around?

22. Tell me about how you dealt with an angry or frustrated customer.

23. How do you organize yourself for day-to-day activities?

24. Tell me about the problems you face in getting all the facets of your job completed on time.

25. What is the biggest mistake you have made in your career?

26. How does your boss get the best out of you?

27. Tell me about the last time you really got angry about a management decision.

28. With what types of employees do you get along best?

29. Tell me some of the ways you have seen managers de-motivate employees.

30. What have you been most criticized as an employee?

31. What do you do when there is a decision to be made and no procedure exists?

32. Tell me about a time when someone lost his or her temper at you in a business environment

33. Tell me about something you started but couldn't finish.

Education

Cover: Elementary school, junior and senior high school, college and university, specialized training, recent courses.

Things to look for: Relevance of schooling

Sufficiency of schooling

Intellectual abilities

Versatility

Breadth and depth of knowledge

Level of accomplishment

Motivation interest

Reaction to authority

Leadership

Teamwork

Ask:

34. I see you went to (school/university) could you tell me about your education there?

35. How would you describe your academic accomplishments?

36. Why did you choose _____ as an area of study?

37. How did you decide to become a (career/job)?

38. What subjects did you enjoy most? Why?

39. What subjects did you find less enjoyable? Why?

40. What were your best subjects at school/university? Why?

41. What subjects did you not do quite so well in? Why?

42. Tell me about any additional training or education you've had since you graduated from school/university?

43. How do you think high school/college contributed to your overall development?

44. What are your plans for further education?

Job Knowledge

Cover: Candidate's knowledge and expectation of job

Things to look for: Vitality

Management of time, energy, and money

Maturity and judgment

Intellectual growth

Cultural breadth

Diversity of interests

Social interests

Social skills

Leadership

Basic values and goals

Situational factors

Ask:

45. I know you don't (or do) have a great deal of information about it, but what is your perception of the job of (job applied for)?

46. I see you've worked as a _____. Would you describe some of your experiences?

47. What problems did you encounter in your position as _____?

48. What qualities do you think it would take to become a successful (job applied for)?

49. What would you say are some of the problems a supervisor has to face?

50. When you consider your skills as a professional, what area concerns you most about your ability to _____?

51. How does this job relate to the overall goals of the company?

52. Explain your understanding of this job's responsibilities.

53. If you were hiring someone for this position, what would you be looking for?

54. What do you expect out of this job?

55. Where do you think you could make the biggest contribution to this organization?

Personal Factors and Outside Activities

Cover: Things to look for: Accuracy of knowledge and realistic job expectations.

Special interest and hobbies

Civic and Community affairs

Living Arrangements

Marriage and family

Finances

Health and energy

Geographical preferences

Ask:

56. In general, how would you describe yourself?

57. Describe the sort of career path you would like to follow.

58. Tell me about your career goals and what kind of things you are looking for in a job.

59. What are some things in a job that are important to you?

60. What would you say there is about this job you're applying for that is particularly appealing to you?

61. What are some things that might not be so desirable?

62. Earlier we were talking about your accomplishments as a _____. What would you say accounted for that success?

63. How about the other side of the coin? What sort of personal qualities and abilities would you like to improve in yourself?

64. What traits or qualities do you most admire in a supervisor?

65. What disappointments, setbacks, or failures have you had in life?

66. What kind of situations make you feel tense and nervous?

67. What are your salary expectations coming into this job?

68. Can you describe a difficult obstacle you've had to overcome? How did you handle it?

69. What do you consider to be your greatest achievement? Why?

70. How do you feel about traveling/working overtime?

71. How do you feel about the right to strike for workers in essential services?

72. Tell me about your recreational or leisure time and interests.

73. You seem to be involved in a number of outside activities. Could you tell me about them?

74. I notice you're involved in_____. Would you tell me about that?

75. Besides_____ what do you like to do with your leisure time?

76. What do you like to avoid getting involved in during your spare time?

77. How do you like to spend your vacations?

78. If you had more time, are there any activities you'd like to participate in? Why?

79. How necessary is it to be creative in your job?

80. What do you consider a good day's effort?

81. What special characteristics should I consider about you as a person?

82. When the pressure is on, where does your extra energy come from?

83. How often do you find it necessary to go above and beyond the call of duty?

84. Give me an example of your initiative in a challenging situation.

85. When do customers/fellow employees really try your patience?

86. What do you feel are your personal limitations?

87. How do you rank among your peers?

88. How do you turn things around when the initial impression of you is bad?

89. What business or social situations make you feel awkward?

90. What kind of rewards are most satisfying to you?

91. What are some of the things you have found especially motivating over the years?

92. What kinds of decisions are most difficult for you?

93. How do you deal with disagreements with others?

94. How important to you are communication and interaction with the staff?

95. How would you describe the ideal job for you?

96. How do you define a successful career?

97. What can you do for us that someone else can't?

98. What do you see as some of your most pressing development needs?

99. What have you been involved with that you now regret?

100. What have the disappointments of life taught you?

101. Why should I hire you?

Overcoming Interview Errors:

In any employment interview, there is a possibility for error. Three typical interviewer errors are: 1) creating a barrier to effective communication; 2) asking sensitive questions at an inappropriate time; and 3) rating errors. The following section will explore these errors and offer insights as to how they might be overcome.

1. Barriers to Effective Communication:

   There are many possible barriers to effective communications that if allowed to go unchecked can lead to interview errors. The four most common barriers to effective communication are listed below.

   Stress: The interviewer may be under a certain amount of stress because of the sense of urgency to identify the right applicant, and then make a good impression on him or her. Usually, though, the applicant feels significantly more stress; their career and financial security are often at stake.

   Defensiveness: If an applicant feels criticized or attacked by the interviewer, they will counter by resisting the perceived offence. Not only will the applicant resist offering the specific information which would prove the interviewer correct, but they may feel compelled to go a step further by stretching the truth in order to disprove the interviewer. Many applicants, once they become defensive, continue a pattern of resistance that impedes in-depth communication.

Poor Listening: Often, communication is hampered because we hear what we expect to hear, rather than what is actually being said. We listen only for what fits our purposes, or until we have "classified" the speaker's remarks in our mind. Ineffective listening habits have probably destroyed the flow of communication in interviews more often than any other single error.

Language Difficulties: The words which are chosen by one communicator must have the same approximate meaning to the other, or communication will be faulty. In many interviews, communication lines have been tenuous because the interviewer's vocabulary was over the head of the candidate, or because words with emotional connotations were interpreted differently by the sender and receiver.

2.   Asking Sensitive Questions at an Inappropriate Time:

In verbal communication, timing is very important. Questions or comments that the applicant may take in stride at one point in the interview may be entirely inappropriate at another point. Especially in the early stages of the interview, emotional barriers can be created by questions on a subject that is sensitive to the applicant. If the interviewer attempts an in-depth exploration of a sensitive subject before the applicant is ready to open up, stress and resistance can set in, and the flow of communication may be adversely affected for the remainder of the interview. For this reason, start the interview with subjects of interest to the candidate. Later on, after the candidate has become more comfortable, it's often possible to probe the more sensitive areas with a minimum of resistance on the candidate's part.

Most questions that are too direct or too sensitive can be asked if they're "softened" by wording them differently. Ask the question you want to ask, but not in a way that is too personal, challenging or threatening.

3. Rating Errors:

    The interview's effectiveness can be greatly undermined by rating errors. The five most common rating errors are: Central Tendency, Halo Effect, Leading Questions, Personal Biases, and Interviewer Domination.

    Central Tendency: refers to the interviewer's inclination to appraise the candidate at a central point on a scale usually the average or midpoint. This is both the most common and most serious type of error. It can result from the fear of rating too high or too low; it seems safer to cluster all scores towards the center. Thus, the interviewer avoids making the "wrong" determination about a candidate, and also protects themselves from appearing biased.

    Halo Effect: occurs when the interviewer's evaluation is based on limited information. Consider: An applicant with a pleasant smile and a firm handshake is sized up as a leading candidate before the interview begins, or an interviewer mentally rejects an applicant who walks in wearing blue jeans.

    Leading Questions: Are evident when interviewers who send out subtle messages which alert the candidate to the desired answer, by the way the question is phrased, are committing another type of error. For example: "Do you think customers are important?" or "Do you think you'll like this kind of work?"

    Personal Biases: Occurs when interviewers who harbor prejudice against specific groups are influenced by personal bias. This is in direct violation of human rights legislation. An interviewer who believes that some jobs are only for men, and others are only for women, is guilty of this error.

    Interviewer Domination: Happens when interviewers who use the interview to oversell the applicant, brag about their own successes or the importance of their own job, or carry on a social conversation instead of an interview, are guilty of interviewer domination errors.

After successful completion of the interviewing stage of the recruiting process you should have identified the best person for the position. The final step is to make the job offer and have both parties agree upon the compensation package. The remaining three chapters of this book focus on the issue of retaining great people. There is a common saying in business that, "leadership is everything" in my opinion this is particularly true in the retention of an organization's people. Chapter five discusses how to become an exceptional leader and the impact of leadership on team retention.

Chapter FIVE

Becoming an Exceptional Leader

*L*et's get rid of management. I think one of the most significant things that corporate America can do during these turbulent and highly competitive times is to get rid of management. What do I mean by this?

I really believe that people don't want to be managed. They want to be led. Whoever heard of a "world manager?" A "world leader," sure. An education leader? Yes. A political leader, a religious leader, a sports leader, a community leader, a labor leader, a business leader, a retail leader ... the point is these people lead, they don't manage.

The carrot always wins over the stick. Ask your horse. My twist on the cliche, you can "lead" your horse to water, but you cannot "manage" him to drink. "If you want to manage somebody, manage yourself." If you do that well, you'll be ready to stop managing and start leading.

One of the challenges of putting all the focus into managing people, as opposed to leading people is that it relies too much on the leader's ability to babysit others and not allow the team to be accountable for their own actions. Rather, it makes a lot more sense if you hire good people, orient and train them and create a motivational climate from which they can grow and learn. Then the people can manage themselves. The key to effective leadership is to lead the organization in a manner that allows everyone to manage themselves.

My definition of leadership is, "the ability to turn a dream or a vision of a desired future state into a reality with the support and assistance of other people."

Another way to look at leadership is to compare it to gardening. Gardeners use sunlight, water, fertilizer and good soil to turn seeds into wonderful plants. Leaders use communication, self-esteem, vision, recognition, rewards and their own personal and organizational goals to help their team reach their potential. Leaders, then, can be seen as the gardeners of corporate America. As Bernard Montgomery once said, "The true test of leadership is the feeling that people have after a chat with you. " By this he means that if after speaking to you (the leader) they (the team) have a feeling of uplift and confidence, you have succeeded as a leader.

There are six commonly accepted myths of leadership that I want to dispel:

Leadership Myth Number 1:

Leadership is a Rare Skill

I don't think leadership is a rare skill. In fact, as I look around, I see all sorts of day-to-day examples of leadership in practice. For example, you can go to your average ice hockey rink and see all sorts of parents volunteering their time after hours, on the weekends, and at the wee hours of the morning, leading youngsters in games of basketball. You see it on the baseball field, in swimming pools, gymnasiums, dance halls, everywhere. That's only one example. There are also examples of people getting involved in a number of leadership roles within a volunteer organization, like the president of the local Toastmaster's Chapter. They could also be leading a fundraising drive for the Heart and Stroke Foundation or some other charitable organization. I think you need to take the time to look around at pure leadership roles. You'll find that indeed there is an abundance of these skills. The challenge is to learn how to transfer the leadership abilities we use in other facets of our lives, and apply them to our business lives.

Leadership Myth Number 2:

Leaders are Born

Another common leadership myth is that leaders are born, and not made. Instead, it's a combination of our life experiences—our environment—as well as our reference groups—people like our parents, our siblings, our friends, the whole education system, religious organizations and the media that create what I call the Reference Groups. Now our Reference Groups become a critical part of our environment. The things that we're exposed to at a young age have a tremendous impact on how we perceive the world. Leaders are not born; rather, they are created as a result of their experiences and their expectations of life, as well as what they've learned from their Reference Groups.

Leadership Myth Number 3:

Leadership is the Same Thing as Management

Managers attempt to *do things right*—according to rules, policies, regulations, and systems—and leaders simply try to *do the right thing*. I see management as the day-to-day supervision of the systems and the people of an organization, while I see leadership as the deliberate energy that is put into an organization to get all the players to jump together as a cohesive team and propel them forward towards the stated short and long-term goals of the organization.

Leadership Myth Number 4:

Leadership Only Exists at The Top

Leadership only exists at the top of an organization is not accurate at all. In some cases, there isn't a lot of leadership at the top of an organization, rather leadership is pervasive throughout the organization. For example, you can be looking at a shop steward who represents the union. This person might be sitting at the bottom of the actual hierarchy chart of the organization, but has real and legitimate power and a bonafide leadership role as a shop steward.

There are leaders within the department, leaders within divisions, leaders within workgroups, and leaders in various projects within an organization. So, I believe that leadership is not a function of someone sitting on the corporate totem pole; rather, leadership is the person making a conscious decision to take an active role within the organization.

Leadership Myth Number 5:

Leadership Power is a Bad Thing

Power is neither a good thing nor a bad thing, it's your intentions as a leader that will create positive or negative results. If you have honorable intentions to do positive things within the organization then I say that power base is actually a positive thing. Now, if you're going to use your power for personal greed or to do a hostile takeover of a corporation, then I see your use of power as negative.

But as I said, leadership power is definitely not a bad thing. In fact, quite the contrary. As leaders, you need to deliberately attempt to expand your personal power base. Because what is power? Power is really the ability to influence others. And one of the things that you're trying to do is influence the majority of individuals within the organization to come on board and share your common vision, and with you lead the company in the direction that you feel the company needs to go.

Adapted from John C. Maxwell's "Five Levels of Leadership"

Level 5: Person/ Respect Based Influence – The Crusader

Level 4: Personal Development Based Influence – The Mentor

Level 3: Production/ Results Based Influence – The Pace-Setter

Level 2: Permission/ Relationship Based Influence – The Friend

Level 1: Position/ Job Description Based Influence – The Boss

Degree of Influence   Success of Organization

Myth Number 6:

Leaders are Only Created by Extraordinary Events

There need not be a shocking or traumatic occurrence to propel people into the position of leadership. Well, you've certainly read about those cases or seen them dramatized in TV shows. But there are many unsung heroes, day-to-day leaders who weren't catapulted into this position, rather it was their own daily dissatisfaction with the events within a current industry or organization that prompted them to take certain actions. As a result, the road they chose led them to the top and they assumed the leadership position.

To be an effective leader in today's business world, you need to possess most, if not all, of the following 10 Dominant Characteristics:

1. Dominant Characteristic: Sense of Purpose

    The first dominant characteristic is what I call a strong sense of purpose. By this I mean that you have a burning desire from within. For example, Thomas Edison is known as one of the most prolific inventors of all time. Apparently, he had a hard time with his invention of the light bulb. He tried thousands of different combinations of materials to get the experiment right, and each combination would either not light up at all or would light up too quickly and explode.

    One night, as the story goes, he was expressing some of his frustration with his experiments to a colleague, when a young man who had been listening to the conversation interjected: "Pardon me, Mr. Edison, sorry for interrupting, but as I listen to you recount your trials and tribulations with this experiment, it strikes me that you failed about 2,000 times to figure out how to make this thing work, so why don't you just give up? Your valuable time is better used doing something else."

    Well, Edison thought about this for a moment, looked at the young man, and replied: "Young man, you don't understand much about the ways of the world. You see, I did not fail 2,000 times. Rather, I was successful in learning 2,000 ways that this will not work. Which means I am that much closer to finding out the way that it will work."

    This illustrates a very important point—that one of the true characteristics of the effective leader is a very strong sense of purpose. It's what I and many others call the burning desire in the pit of the stomach.

Another example is Henry Ford. Back in the 1920's, when everyone else was making a few cars, he said, "Well, what if I could produce a car and make it dependable and everything else that the consumer wanted. If I could produce enough of those, I could make a lot of money as well as take care of the transportation requirements for the vast majority of Americans."

So, he went out and talked to a number of American consumers, and asked them what they were looking for in an automobile. They in turn told him a number of different physical characteristics, safety issues, and how fast it should go, and so on and so forth. Ford brought all the findings back to his team of engineers, mechanics and designers and told them to build a car possessing all of the requirements detailed by the American consumer. Furthermore, Mr. Ford added, that the car had to be built within a specific budget. None of the team believed it was possible. Ford's reaction was to fire them all and hire a whole new team of engineers, designers, and mechanics.

Because of this burning desire, and personal belief that the Ford Company could do it, Henry Ford surrounded himself with similar people who accepted his vision. In turn, they changed the rules. They created a whole new methodology for building cars—the assembly line: mass production.

The major point of difference between the average person and the leader is that the average person cannot believe it until he/she sees it. Whereby the leader says, "If I believe it, then I'll see it." It's having that passion, that sense of purpose, that makes a leader of an ordinary person.

With more than eighteen years of experience training people in leadership principles, in 41 countries around the world, I've studied thousands of men and women from all walks of life. My research has brought about many interesting facts about purpose that I would like to share with you.

One of the most striking facts is that those who have succeeded in their endeavors applied common principles very effectively. In turn, these people became uncommon leaders in their various fields. One funny thing about common sense though, is that it's not that common anymore.

You know, it's not enough for people to have education, intelligence, or the ability to succeed. Thousands of leaders throughout the world have all these traits but still fail, or produce at performance levels far lower than their potential. Why? Because they lack worthy ambition. People without a purpose never leave a mark on the world. They're lost in the mass of people, and they do not bring out their true talents and potential. Whatever initial advantages these people may have, without the primary principal purpose, they become poor—or at best average—at the performance. Life is too short for any one of us to accomplish everything. However, some of us, if we apply our potential, can accomplish more than one thing well in our lives. Many, in fact, can accomplish at least one important worthy purpose in life if we set our minds to do so.

Success comes to those leaders who have a definite purpose in their lives and are supported by practical written plans of action and strategies of how they're going to accomplish this. We all must have a specific mission which can contribute positively to other people. This primary mission needs to be bigger and broader than our own self. The following questions can get you thinking about your life mission:

- What do you want out of life?
- What is your life mission?
- What becomes of you when you have achieved your life's mission?
- Which category out of the following six categories are you striving to accomplish?

    1) The challenge of life.

    2) The love for people.

3) The well-being of others.

4) Their personal wealth.

5) The power over other people.

6) The status of personal health and well-being.

- Can your present situation help you achieve this major goal?

- Do you have a well-written plan to work towards this major goal?

It is only when you can answer the above questions truthfully that you will be able to aim for something meaningful in life. Don't settle for a mere mediocre sort of existence. Don't measure yourself by your past failures or achievements, nor by your present abilities.

Make a cause more important than yourself your purpose in life. For example, take Japanese Doctor Yushero Nagamatz—a very famous inventor. To date he's registered more than 2,360 patents to his name. He does this by working 9 a.m. to midnight each day of his life. Dr. Nagamatz says, "I have a mission to accomplish in life. Japan is very short of any resources, beyond people, water and fish, and must import all goods critical to industry. Therefore, if we don't create, we shall die."

With such a purpose in his life, it is little wonder that he has been inducted into the International Inventors' Hall of Fame by the Inventors' Club of America, and he has won the Blue Ribbon Award for inventors.

Another example is Mother Teresa. She had a life mission—to help poor people in India who were sick and dying by the thousands. When she first started her personal crusade, she faced many problems and obstacles. She has sponsored many hospitals, schools, and places of dwelling for the poor of India. A Nobel Peace Prize winner, she has said, "Each one of us has a mission to fulfill, our mission of love. At the hour of death, when we come face to face with God, we are measured by love. Not how much we have done, but how much we have loved, and how much love we have put into our actions."

The burning desire to achieve your ambitions is such a strong, deep, emotional urge of wanting to achieve a worthy goal that you are prepared to pay any price to achieve it. Exceptional leaders possess strong will-power to get what they want, and they're willing to pay the price in advance to get it. Therefore, they succeed in achieving their goals. Most people wish for many things, but they're not willing to pay the price for what they want. Hence, they give up when faced with problems and obstacles and invariably sabotage their success.

A strong will-power to win is reflected by one of my colleagues, W. Mitchell. He is a professional speaker who tours around the country with a very simple yet powerful message. "It's not what happens to you, it's what you do about it."

Some 25 years ago, young Mitchell was working in San Francisco on the trolley cars. A horrific motorcycle accident left him with burns to 90 percent of his body, and broken bones. After several weeks of soul-searching and going through the "Why me Lord?" syndrome, he decided that he wasn't going to dwell on the negative, but rather say to himself, "Well, what do I do now'? What do I wait for?"

Several years later, Mitchell, the founder and major shareholder of Vermont Castings, one of the world's leading producers and exporters of wood burning stoves, had become quite wealthy. A few years later, while flying his small aircraft with two friends around Colorado they had a freakish accident. While his two friends were able to walk away from the wreck, he was an instant paraplegic. His wife, unable to deal with this tragedy, left him. Again, he went through all the agony of what I call, "The Victim Mentality" saying, "Why, Lord? Why has this happened to me? This is such a terrible thing. I feel terrible." However, after a while, he decided to focus on what he did have versus what he didn't have.

With that in mind, he later became the Mayor of a small community in Colorado. He took on a major mining exploration company that wanted to exploit the natural resources of a nearby mountain, and became known as the man who saved the mountain. He also ran for State Governor and, although he didn't win, he came in a close second. He now tours all over the world with his very motivational subject, entitled "It's not what happens to you, it's what you do about it." I think his message is very powerful; it needs to be heard by many, many people.

W. Mitchell's strong will-power to win is a definite indicator of someone who's a true inspiration to us all; he is definitely a contemporary leader.

How can we take the burning desire that we all have within us and multiply it? Well, there are two proven techniques. One is called Creative Visualization, and another method is called Positive Affirmation Statements.

With Creative Visualization, you're creating a mental picture of yourself achieving your goals to become the kind of person and leader that you want. If you perform this mental exercise, this visualization in your mind, for two or three minutes every night before going to sleep and every morning when you get up, you will see yourself actually being more successful in becoming the leader that you want to become. You will have the impact on your followers that you want to have. You will also create an emotional link with this success.

Positive Affirmation Statements is talking about your own level of self-talk, to program yourself with more confidence in your own abilities. You can do this to remind yourself when you say, "I am a great leader. I am a visionary." See it in your mind and repeat it over and over again. What you end up doing is creating and planting a number of positive thoughts in the subconscious mind so that you actually move towards success more rapidly.

2. Dominant Characteristic: Persistence

    Here is a great example of persistence as a dominant characteristic of an effective leader. Towards the latter part of World War II, in the United Kingdom, Sir Winston Churchill gathered a number of people. He was going to make a speech. The German Air Force was bombing London and the surrounding area, almost winning the air battle. At this point Churchill decided that he needed to inspire his people to get them excited and working towards one goal. He told them the key to succeeding was persistence. He summed up one of his most famous speeches with a very short but powerful conclusion: "Never give up. Never, never give up." In those seven words Sir Winston Churchill epitomized the power of persistence; to create a sense of the unstoppable.

    Brian Tracy, professional speaker and author of the best-selling Nightingale-Conant audio cassette, says, "To create an unstoppable mindset, leaders must be persistent." Former president Hubert Hoover said, "Nothing in the world can take the place of persistence. Talent will not: nothing is more common than unsuccessful people with talent. Genius will not: unrewarded genius is almost a proverb. Education will not: the world is full of educated derelicts. The slogan 'Press on' has solved—and always will solve—the problems of the human race."

3. Dominant Characteristic: Self-knowledge

    Self-knowledge is knowing what your strengths and weaknesses are. A great exercise to do is to take a blank piece of paper and on the left side write down all of your strengths, on the right side your weaknesses. Be as accurate and honest as you can, invite someone who knows you well to review and add to your list. The final and most important exercise is to identify specific weaknesses that you commit to addressing and to come up with an action plan for self improvement.

4. Dominant Characteristic: The Learning Mindset

    "The Learning Mindset" is having the student mentality. The student mentality is essentially recognizing that you know a little bit about the subject matter, but you will seek more information and always try to learn more.

The following diagram shows the four levels of learning.

4 Levels of Learning

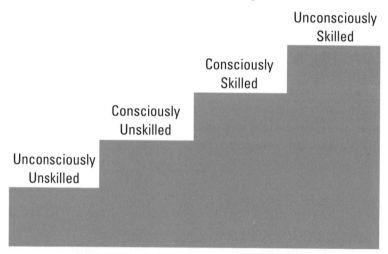

The bottom level of learning is called "Unconsciously Unskilled." In the Unconscious/ Unskilled stage of learning, you are not aware that you do not know. Then at some point, someone, or something brings it to your attention that you do not know. So then you now become conscious of the fact that you are unskilled, and then you move into Stage 2, where you become "Consciously Unskilled."

At this point, you are bothered by the fact that you do not know, so you start to do something about it. You take courses, you read books, you learn. And then you move into Stage 3, where you now become "Consciously Skilled." This can be a very dangerous stage. This is what I often call "The Brightest Stage." At this stage, you believe that you know everything that there is to know about the subject of which you're talking. Obviously, if you start to believe that you know everything about the subject matter, you're going to stop investing yourself, and you're going to stop learning. I think one of the key things here is to get out of this state. It's enough to remember that the good Lord provided you with two ears and only one mouth, so that you may listen twice as much as you speak. What do I mean by this? When I'm speaking, I'm not learning. As soon as I take the time to close my mouth and listen, then I can learn more.

And that leads into Stage 4. If you are the true master, you're constantly seeking to learn more, constantly immersing yourself in additional knowledge, eventually you will become unconsciously skilled. You know your unconscious skills when, for example, you're playing goalie in a soccer game, and all of a sudden there's a flurry of action, and you've lost sight of who has the ball. Then out of your peripheral vision you see the ball racing toward you. Purely out of instinct you jump up to deflect the ball. That's an example of someone who has become a master. The person has trained so much, learned so much about the technique, and has created an unconscious reflex that, in this case, will prevent a goal from being scored.

5. Dominant Characteristic: Joy in Work
    Effective leaders don't see themselves as going to work, rather, they have a total sense of pleasure and joy in relation to their work. That's why they're able to expend such a phenomenal amount of time and energy into their careers. In many cases, they see it as going to play, and they just happen to get paid for playing. You have to have an absolute passion for what you do in order to be the very best at it. If you are used to staring at the clock, punching out at 5:00 p.m. sharp, and all that nine-to-five mentality, then you can never truly become an effective leader. To rise above the mediocrity of life and be a successful leader, you must be a person of action; you must be willing to work with consistent and continuous effort.

Former Chief Justice Harold E. Hughes put it very clearly by saying, "I believe in work. Hard work and long hours of work. No one has a break down from overwork, but from worry and inactivity. "

Extraordinary leaders are actually ordinary people who put in extraordinary effort in their pursuit of excellence. Many people do not like their work, and only some people like their work moderately. There are very few who actually love their work. For example, workers usually toil with an indifferent attitude, while great artists create their work with unquenchable passion and care. When you're engaged in work you love, you can invest long hours without feeling tired or fatigued. You become most efficient and you succeed better when you love your work and are committed and dedicated to your loved ones, organization, and country.

6. Dominant Characteristic: Golden Rule

    The effective leader seeks to develop loving, nurturing, supportive relationships with other humans. The Golden Rule in human relationships states, "Do unto others as you want others to do unto you." In Christianity, Jesus said, "All things whatsoever that men should do to you, do so to them." In Islam, "No one of you is a believer until you desire for his brother that which he has desired for himself." In Buddhism, "Hurt not others in ways that you yourself would find hurtful." In Hinduism, "Do not unto others that which would cause you pain if done unto you."

    There are always references to the "self-made leader." In fact, there's no such thing as the self-made leader, because no leader has ever made it to the top without the help of other people. It has been said, "He rises highest who helps others to rise." Just like milk, you can never stop the cream from rising to the top. You can never rise above mediocrity until you possess distinguished hallmarks of effective leadership. In business, sports, or in personal life, there's going to be ups and there's going to be downs. It's when you're down and sometimes out that you need your friends.

All these metaphors may sound cliche but the truth is you need friends and colleagues to encourage you and help you come up again. Even if you're a leader of a group of people, you need a collective and united effort to achieve your goal as well as the group members' own personal goals. This is only possible when you're able to assert a friendly and effective relationship with each and every one of them in order to build a unified team. You can be rich only when you enrich the lives of other people. You only learn the meaning of living when you can surrender your ego to the service of your fellow person. In order to be of sincere interest to others, you must first be a sincere friend. As a colleague of mine, founder of the National Speakers' Association, Cavett Robert has often said, "No one cares how much you know until they know how much you care." You can live in history when you think more of your friends than of yourself, your country rather than your bank book. Real and true friends will follow you anywhere; through the brightness and the darkness, through the shadows and the sunlight. Ask yourself these thought-provoking questions: How many true friends, and not just social friends, do I really have? Who are they? Do they believe in me? Do they encourage me to become an outstanding leader in my specialized field? Will they lend me a helping hand, or even two hands, if I need it? Do they encourage me and motivate me to achieve my goals in life?

Here are some useful tips that can help you apply the Golden Rule principle and develop true friendship, co-operation, and support other people as you become an even more effective leader.

    a. Be more lovable to your loved ones. Spend quality time in meaningful activities with them.

    b. Be more concerned about your fellow workers and help them achieve their personal goals. Introduce a more caring attitude for them by letting them participate in the decision-making process, by making them feel a part of the organization.

c. Associate with successful people, particularly those that are the leaders in your profession and industry and then you learn from their experiences. In my case, if I want to become even more successful as a professional speaker, I need close personal friends who are well-known professional speakers. I have asked people like Bill Gibson, Brian Tracy, and the late Og Mandino to personally be my mentor.

d. Apply "The customer comes first" and "The customer is always right" principles to your clientele. Always be prepared to serve them sincerely and efficiently.

The Servant

"Humility recognizes that the only master there is on earth is a servant. All those who seek to become masters fail. So few are seeking to become servants, and it is the servant who others eventually call master. This is true of everyone who at sometime or another has been named master. The master is always working twenty hours a day while the disciple is sleeping his eight hours and enjoying holidays."—
Bill Gibson.

e. Form a team of professionals in various specialized skills to advise and support you to achieve your mission. These experts may include: a doctor, a dentist, a lawyer, a banker, a tax accountant, a business investment consultant, a spiritual adviser, a personal confidante, your own success coach/ mentor, or an insurance agent.

7. Dominant Characteristic: Calculated Risks

An effective leader is willing to take calculated risks and is prepared to experiment. The leader is prepared—as they say in Star Trek—"To boldly go where no one has gone before." This is not to say, take unnecessary, dangerous tangents; rather look at the whole opportunity, size up the situation, and say "Okay, can I take a calculated risk here?"

8. Dominant Characteristic: Opportunities

    An effective leader is someone who sees problems as opportunities. Basically, it's how you choose to see the world. Are you going to look at every little setback or every little obstacle as a failure, and then remind yourself that you failed in that area? Or are you going to look at all these times that maybe you weren't as successful as you would have liked to have been, as learning opportunities, and an opportunity for you to go forward? Remember Thomas Edison.

9. Dominant Characteristic: Living Magnet

    You draw people, places, and circumstances into your life that are consistent with your dominant thoughts. So if you are a very positive, upbeat, proactive, successful person, you will draw those types of people into your life, and into your organization. There's a real magnetism or charisma that is exuded by the effective leader. And this doesn't necessarily have to be done in a very loud or forceful manner. You can take a very quiet, self-assured priest, or an individual like Mahatma Ghandi. Now there's someone who exuded all sorts of personal power and charisma without having to raise his voice or lift a loaded weapon. It's like a magnet that draws people in towards you. And one of the things of course, for the leader, is he/she has to have a sufficient number of followers to help move the leader towards his/her stated goals.

10. Dominant Characteristic: Serve Others

    The effective leader constantly seeks to serve the needs of other people. What you want to accomplish in the long run is the empowerment of every individual within the organization to the degree that everyone is actually managing his/her day-to-day action as each individual moves towards the long-term objectives of the organization. But how do we get to this stage? The Leadership Success Chart following the survey specifically explains how leaders can empower individuals within their organization.

Leadership Success Model

Vision + Communication + Positioning + Self-Management = Empowerment

What does the above model mean? This can be seen as taking the time to paint a mental picture of a desired state into your mind. Now your vision can come from the mission statement of the organization. John F. Kennedy had a vision in the early 60's to have an American on the moon by the end of the decade. Martin Luther King had a vision of equality among races that was expressed in his slogan, "I have a dream."

By taking the time to help your followers paint a mental picture of the desired statement in their minds, you're going to add a lot more power and conviction behind the mission, behind the objective. When JFK created the vision of an American on the moon, he used all sorts of visual aids to help people buy into this vision. Throughout NASA, there were pictures and symbols of the moon and of lunar exploration, and various pieces of apparatus were left around so people could look at them and visually connect in their minds with the purpose and the dominant theme that was bringing them together in the organization and propelling them forward.

There are seven key points that leaders strive to communicate to their followers. The first is their absolute passion for their vision. This is expressed by the leader's energy, by his/her commitment, and by his/her own modeling of the desired state. They are living the model, as it were.

The second point is leaders want their vision to be understood by all people, by all of their followers. Thirdly, the leader wants everyone within the organization to understand what's in it for each one of them. In other words, what the benefits are to each person in being successful in achieving his/her vision. The fourth point is that leaders seek to communicate solidarity and clarity and unison from senior leaders down. The fifth point is that leaders strive to draw in all their team to the vision so that they are committed in striving towards the achievement of the long-term goal. The sixth point, leaders also seek to communicate action so that the team will be propelled into action. And lastly, the one I think is the real test here, is that interpersonal communications, the relationship between the leader and the followers, will be strengthened.

Sometimes there are barriers that, unless dealt with, will prevent you from being 100 percent successful in achieving your stated vision. They could be internal barriers, external barriers, or relationship barriers.

Internal barriers can be the actual structural recording systems that are used within the organization. External barriers can be legislation, challenges with suppliers, or any other difficulties with clients that could prevent us from achieving our vision. And lastly, probably the most complex barrier is the relationship between the various team players within the organization. What you need to do is find out what obstacles lie within your path and resolve to overcome them and work directly towards success. A key component in leadership success is self-management. If every individual within the organization is held personally accountable for managing him/herself and is given the tools and the latitude to manage him/herself effectively, then no one needs to worry about managing another individual. That would free up the leader's time to do more effective things such as acting as a coach, mentor and leader, rather than playing the role of supervisor and manager.

Five Keys to Self-Management

There are five keys to self-management—and this applies to any level of the organization and to any position within the organization.

1. Positive Mental Attitude

    You need to develop a positive mental attitude. In other words, it's how you choose to see the world. Do you see the world as being a relatively negative place, or a positive place?

    The only things in the world that you have complete control over are your thoughts, your words, your goals and your actions. Positive, rather than negative thoughts, should eventually become the dominant thoughts in your life. But remember, you're always free to change those thoughts. As I have already stressed, you should be programming thoughts into your mind that are consistent with the direction you want to go and the goals you want to achieve.

2. Stress Management

    This is your ability to cope with the ever-growing trend of having to do more with less resources. You can't really manage stress, even though this expression, "stress management," is used all the time. Stress is not some green-eyed, long-tooth hairy monster that waits to pounce on us. Stress is nothing more than an internal reaction to an external event or situation. Chances are you have seen two different people experiencing the very same situation, yet reacting quite differently. One person is freaking out while the other person is looking at it quite calmly and saying, "Hey, what's the big deal?" What you need to do is not manage stress, but manage yourself more effectively and you'll actually endure fewer stress symptoms.

    Stress management is keeping the right perspective. What I mean by this is keeping worry under control. One of the number one stressors in life, is that things can be blown out of proportion. Looking at a whole bunch of scenarios, you can say, "Ah, what if this happens, what if that happens?"

    So, if you're feeling a little stressed, don't worry, just take out a piece of paper and write down "My Worry List for Today." Write down all of your worries and itemize them according to the Worry Chart on the next page. Just by virtue of the fact that you're writing them down, you're forced to focus on your worries, and when you're done you'll say, "Hey, it's not that bad." At the end of doing this exercise take your list and check off the vast majority of worries. These are the ones on which you should be spending time.

    Then you can ask yourself, "Of those that are still left on the list, which ones are likely to happen and, if they do happen, what's the worst possible outcome?" And once you can talk about the worst possible outcome, you'll say, "Well, even that's not so bad. So, why am I spending so much time worrying about it?"

Worry Chart
40% will never happen
30% have already happened
12% health related issues
10% miscellaneous issues
4% no control over
4% real control over

3. Time Management

    Time management you need to look at very closely. It's impossible to manage time. It's like a person who says, "Well, I just saved two hours." How can you save two hours? What did you do? Did you throw it in the bank? It's impossible to save two hours. What you can do is look at the 24 hours that you have each day, and say, "Okay, how can I manage myself with respect to time? How can I be more efficient within the given amount of time that I have? Either in a day, or for the rest of my life."

    When you look at time that way, you can actually take the time and prioritize your most important issues. This is when you need to look at the rule of 80/20. This says, basically, that only 20 percent of all the things you have to focus on contribute to 80 percent of the success of your job. So, what you really need to do is spend 80 percent of your time on the 20 percent of the goals and responsibilities and specific actions that are going to give you an 80 percent return on your investment. One of the ways to do that is to clarify how you prioritize different tasks and activities during the day. This is a very simple time management system that is called the A-B-C-D-E method of prioritization. At the beginning of the day write down all the different tasks that you have to deal with that day; let's say you come up with 30 different tasks. Beside each of those tasks, write down an appropriate letter. If it is absolutely essential to complete the task today, you write down "A," because "A" stands for "absolutely," this must be done today. "B" stands for "beneficial." It would be beneficial, it would be nice to get this done, but it's not absolute. "C" stands for "convenient." It would be convenient to have this done, but it's not beneficial, and it's not absolute. "D" means it should be "delegated." It should be delegated to someone else. Finally "E" it should be "eliminated," it should be thrown in the garbage and never thought of again because it's a time waster.

Next, you go through and list all the different priorities for the day, the different tasks you have to do and rank them according to their priority using the A-B-C-D-E ranking system. This forces you to focus on the 20 percent of the things that are going to make 80 percent difference in your life.

4. Creative Solutions

    Becoming a creative problem solver is to actually see problems as opportunities in clever disguises.

    An average leader is confronted with numerous challenges every day. When a challenge occurs, the leader has two alternatives. He/she must determine if the issue is:

    - not worth solving and forget about it
    - worth some time and effort; then use the seven step guide to creative solutions

The Seven Steps to Creative Solutions

Step 1: Define the Challenge

A challenge exists when there is a significant difference between what is happening and what should be happening.

Step 2: Decide on Its Worth

Situation analysis requires time and energy. A leader will find that some challenges are not important enough to warrant any effort, and they should not devote resources to every issue that surfaces.

Step 3: Find the Facts

Fact finding is conducted for two purposes: to gather data and to test data. You need to ask who, what, when, and where. These questions impose boundaries around the situation that help to discriminate between relevant and irrelevant information. To ensure the quality of information, there are three criteria that must be met:

- Is it accurate? Verify your information. Inaccurate data can lead to an incorrect decision.

- Is it current? Insist on current information.

- Is it complete? Gathering information costs money and has a point of diminishing return. You need a plan for gathering enough, but not too much, information.

Step 4: Identify Alternative Solutions

Once you have isolated a challenge and found it worthy of your time and energy, you must create a solution. Arriving at a decision involves identifying alternative actions and choosing the one that will best yield the desired result. Experience also plays a role in making decisions. Most people overcome challenges each day by making simple, routine decisions. While these habitual solutions often work, you may be overlooking a viable, more effective alternative. This alternative solution could result in a higher level of performance.

Step 5: Specify Important Characteristics

Before you decide on a solution, you should have a clear picture of your ideal situation. One technique is to visualize the perfect solution and list its characteristics. For example, an ideal solution to a production challenge would be one that is inexpensive, uses existing personnel, and does not decrease productivity.

You should list the characteristics for each possible alternative. Then, using the definitions below, you should categorize each characteristic.

- (A's) Absolute Characteristics—those that must be present for an alternative to be selected. If an alternative lacks absolute characteristics, eliminate it as a possibility.

- (B's) Beneficial Characteristics—though desirable, do not have the power of absolutely necessary characteristics.

- (C's) Convenient Characteristics—those that would be nice to have, like decorations on a cake, but they are not necessary. They would just make the solution more appealing.

Step 6: Weigh the Alternatives

Imagine that you are hiring a sales clerk. Review the sales clerk job description and assign weights (A, B, or C) to each specific task identified in the job description. For example: If you felt that greeting customers in a "friendly, open manner" was substantially more important than "filing," you might assign an "A" weight to greeting the customer and a "C" to the filing task.

Step 7: Implement the Decision

There are four steps you can take to increase the likelihood of a satisfactory solution.

1) List the difficulties this solution might encounter.

2) Make face-to-face contact with the people who are most affected by the decision.

- Explain the need for the decision. This can help in motivating employees to carry out the decision.

- Describe the goal. Knowing what the final results will look like can assist people in recognizing progress.

· Involve employees in the plan. Employee's input into the decision-making process not only improves the quality of the decision, but can also increase staff's commitment to the decision.

· Listen to any concerns. Knowing the potential difficulties beforehand often helps you to prevent them.

3) Make certain the people who will implement the decision have adequate resources to do so, for example: time, money, equipment, skills, knowledge, authority, support, and most important of all, the right attitude.

4) Make sure the solution does not:

· violate policy

· interfere with previously established goals or priorities

· cost more than it is worth

· become so rigid that it does not allow any flexibility in its implementation

5. Key to Self-Management: Human Relations Skills

The most important aspect of maintaining superior human relations is the leaders' ability to communicate with their team. Food for thought: "All good leaders are great listeners."

Effective leaders need to be aware of the seven most common barriers to communication:

1. Uncommon symbols or slang. Sometimes we have a tendency to overuse industry jargon. Do not assume that everyone understands what you are talking about.

2. Lack of communications training.

3. Environmental disturbances—excessive background noise or message overload.

4. Improper attitude, assumptions or personal biases.

5. Cultural, educational, or age differences between sender and receiver.

6. The sender/receiver relationship.

7. Speed of thought—the average adult processes words into sentences at approximately 500 words per minute, but can only speak 150 words per minute. The challenge is to stay focused on the meaning of the words and to discipline your mind from wandering.

Another powerful and quick reminder for winning human relations is what I call the rule of 70/30. This rule reminds us that when we are communicating with others we should limit our speaking to 30 percent of the conversation, thus we can listen 70 percent of the time. This is important because it is impossible to learn if we are not listening. Three ways to improve overall effectiveness of communications:

1.Clarity—say exactly what you mean

2.Honesty—say how you feel

3.Directness—say what you want

Note: As the leader you are 100 percent responsible for both sending and receiving the communication.

A Short Course in Human Relations

The 6 most important words:
I admit I made a mistake

The 5 most important words:
You did a good job

The 4 most important words:
What is your opinion

The 3 most important words:
If you please

The 2 most important words:
Thank you

The most important word:
We

The least important word:
I

Chapter SIX

Training and Developing Your Key Resource . . . Your People

One of the biggest reasons most organizations can't seem to retain great people is because they are not fully tapping into the person's potential. Most organizations will say that this is not true, that they have dedicated training departments and training officers. To this argument I respond that it is a step in the right direction but not enough.

Great people have an overwhelming desire to win; they are very committed and will work very hard to succeed. However, it's virtually impossible to succeed alone; these people crave a work environment that fosters their ongoing development. One way to see the difference is to consider the Funk & Wagnall's Dictionary definitions of two words which are commonly treated as meaning the same thing.

Train: To render qualified or obedient by instruction or drill.

Develop: To expand or bring out the potential

Most companies focus on "training" their people to "do" things better, whereas the most progressive organizations "develop" their people to "be" better. I want to be clear that I am not against training; in fact, there can be a tremendous value in increasing one's skills and knowledge base. What I am saying is that development is more holistic in nature in that it aims to assist the individual realize their potential.

The most obvious reason for developing your people is to help them achieve their potential, while equipping them to provide the maximum benefit to the organization. In order for team development to occur you need two key elements; a leader that will act as a mentor while creating a positive learning environment and an individual that is "coachable". A coachable person is someone who is enthusiastic about developing themselves and is open to learning new things.

Six Truths of Adult Learning

The following is a summary of generally accepted truths derived from the laws of adult learning. They can help you to better understand how people learn.

1. People learn at different rates; Trainees differ in background, motivation, work habits and learning ability. Trainers must be ready to adjust to these individual differences. Be prepared to step in with a word of encouragement when a trainee has a bad day or when he/she has trouble coping with difficult material.

2. People learn better when you appeal to all their senses; Trainees will remember better if they "see" as well as "hear" what is being taught. Bring your material alive with examples, illustrations and demonstrations. A vivid, exciting learning experience is more likely to be remembered than a routine or boring one.

3. People need to know when they have done a good job; Positive reinforcement provides the incentive to learn. People accept and repeat those activities that are pleasant and satisfying. A good trainer can make sure every trainee experiences some satisfaction in learning.

4. People learn better by looking at the "big picture" first; Your training will be more effective when you use the whole-part-whole approach. Start your training sessions by

looking at the "big picture" or the entire job first. Then break down the job into its smaller tasks and show how each piece fits into the puzzle. Individual parts of a job should be explained in detail only after your trainees understand the overall job.

5. People learn better if they concentrate on one learning task at a time; too much information will produce anxiety in your trainees.

   Information is better recalled when seven or fewer points are used.

6. People must be given a chance to actually experience the things they have been learning; your training will be more effective when your trainees can practice their new skills on the job. For example, a Loans Officer will learn how to grant a loan much faster by actually doing it than by reading it.

The most straight forward exercise is often overly complicated: the creation of a Personal Development Plan. In fact, it is quite simple. The first step is to review the Job Description. This will layout the specific duties and corresponding areas of skills and knowledge. It will also mention the desired personal characteristics of the ideal job holder. The second step is to fill the blank Personal Development Plan provided below. The key is to prioritize the specific areas of development and to identify the sources of development. This process works best when both the leader and the job holder jointly fill in and commit to the plan. You want to link the fulfillment of the person's dreams and aspirations with the objectives of the organization.

To further illustrate the point I have included a sample Personal Development Plan for a Sales Professional.

Sample Personal Development Plan – Sales Professional

Development Area	Source of Development	Priority
Maintaining a Positive Outlook		
Setting Meaningful Goals		
Learning the Power of Visualization		
Relationship & Rapport Building		
Prospecting Clients		
Powerful Sales Presentations		
Effective Communications		
Stress Management		
Time Management		
Great Openers		
Uncovering Buying Motivators		
Handling Areas of Concern		
Telephone Sales Power		
Obtaining Client Referrals		
Networking		
Maintaining a Positive Attitude		
Professionalism/ Dress		
Finalizing the Transaction		
Collecting the Payment		
After Sale Account Building		
Other		

My Personal Development Plan

Development Area	Source of Development	Priority

Sources of Development

On-the-Job

This is the most common form of training and development; in a nut-shell it means learning while performing.

Mentorship

Mentorship is similar to coaching except that a mentor also shares a form of relationship with the learner. A mentor cares about the mentee's long term success and commits to assist in the "fast-tracking" of the person's development. This is done by the mentor sharing all of the lessons that they themselves have learned over the years. This form of compressed learning can literally shave off many years of learning for the mentee.

Company Training Programs

The value of "in-house" company training programs is two-fold; one the company can ensure a standardized method of sharing the same message to everyone on the team, while the second is that in certain circumstances no one understands the uniqueness of the company better than itself.

Corporate Retreats/ Meetings

One of the most effective development tools is to have ongoing team meetings. These meetings provide an excellent opportunity to share new ideas, products or services with the team. By having an upbeat meeting it will be motivating for all in attendance. Leaders should share their insights with the group so that others can learn from their experiences. Top producers and innovators should be publicly recognized and rewarded for their achievements. This encourages the entire team to strive for better results.

External Seminars, Workshops and Conferences

There are numerous seminars, workshops and conferences going on at any given time in most cities in America. They can be offered by Associations, Chambers of Commerce, Universities and Institutes as well as by private seminar companies. Some are open to the public while others are exclusive members. The presenters can be consultants, university professors, successful local business leaders, or internationally acclaimed authors, speaking on a wide variety of topics. Some of these presenters also offer customized workshops tailored to the specific needs to the client.

CD's, Videos, Audio Tapes and Books

One of the best ideas is to invest in your own development at your own pace. CD's, videos, audio tapes and books are the best sources for low cost, self development programs. You can purchase these development products at book stores, mail order catalogues, training company websites, or you can borrow them from public libraries, board of trade, university libraries or the company training department.

New Recruit Orientation

Approximately one out of every five people in America and Canada will quit or be fired this year.

This means that an average 90,000 people will be starting a new position each business day of this year.

One of the primary reasons that people change jobs is that they were never made to feel welcome as a part of the team when they joined. Another big issue is that many people get hired and only have vague notions of what performance is expected of them. As a result, the new recruit never really feels connected with the company and his/her original high level of energy soon drops to a level of apathy. Once this occurs, the company will quickly fire the individual to "cut its losses." In other cases the person, feeling that it is a useless struggle, decides to quit his/her job and try his/her luck elsewhere. Once this happens, the company that he/she just left is once again confronted with the need to find, hire and train someone else.

The role of effective orientation is to assist the new recruit to become productive as quickly as possible while maintaining the person's initial level of interest and enthusiasm.

Although orientation costs time and money, to most organizations these costs are sound investments. Newly-hired recruits are seldom capable of fully performing their job duties. Even individuals with experience need to learn about the organization—its people, its policies, and its procedures. They may need training in order to perform successfully. The gap between the new recruit's abilities and the job's demands can be substantial.

A new recruit's orientation program can reduce turnover and save an organization thousands of dollars and hundreds of hours of putting out fires.

Whether a company has two team members or 20,000 the orientation of new recruits should never be left to chance. A thorough, well planned, effectively executed orientation is an integral part in keeping your team productive and happy.

Benefits of New Recruit Orientation

Helps keep new recruits HAPPY by making them:

- feel at ease and welcomed;
- feel good about the company; and
- feel comfortable with their decision.

Helps keep new recruits PRODUCTIVE by:

- explaining standard of performance;
- teaching basics;
- being a starting point for training and development;
- reducing mistakes and saving time; and
- reducing turnover.

Most new recruits start off with a great deal of energy, enthusiasm and excitement. They are eager to prove to their leader that they were a good hiring decision. The atmosphere created during the orientation program can greatly affect what happens to this person's level of interest. A quality orientation will help the recruit feel good about the opportunity.

With the new recruit feeling at ease and welcomed, his/her decision to join the company will be positively reinforced. In a nutshell, the biggest benefit's of orientation is the happiness the team feels.

The second major benefit of orientation is an increase in productivity. Ken Blanchard, in his book *The One Minute Manager*, talks of how he believes in passing out the final exam during the first day of his class. Blanchard does this because he wants his students to understand right from day one what performance standards are expected. By spelling out what is expected, you reduce stress that is caused by role ambiguity. New recruits can focus on activities that are important. The net result is lower stressed, task driven, highly productive people.

Part of an effective orientation is taking the time to ensure that the new recruit can do the basic tasks. It is important to build first upon the similar tasks, then master them prior to moving on. New recruit orientation is not difficult, nor does it consume a lot of time if done right.

A poorly planned or non-existent orientation can quickly undo all the previous efforts of recruiting and selection as one more person travels through the "revolving door" of personnel. Turnover can be greatly reduced by a well-thought-out orientation program. The results will be fewer mistakes and a better understanding of what is expected. This should lead to improved customer service, higher productivity and improved team morale. Everyone wins—you, the recruit, the organization and, most of all, the real bosses of any company, your customers or clients.

Given human nature, we often tend to imitate what we have experienced. If you received a good orientation in the past, chances are you will conduct your orientation in a similar manner. Similarly, if your orientation was poor, then this chapter can help you develop a positive orientation program.

How Well Have You Done in the Past?

Think for a moment about the last few recruits your organization hired, then honestly answer the questions on the following page.

	Employee		
	1	2	3
Name:	_____	_____	_____
1. How long has each person been on board?	_____	_____	_____
2. Was the new recruit made to feel welcome?	Yes No	Yes No	Yes No
3. Do you think the recruit regrets the decision to join your organization?	Yes No	Yes No	Yes No
4. Was the person productive within a short period of time?	Yes No	Yes No	Yes No
5. Did your organization have a planned orientation program?	Yes No	Yes No	Yes No
6. If you had been in the recruit's place, would you have been satisfied with the orientation?	Yes No	Yes No	Yes No
7. Did you routinely take time to get to know the recruit?	Yes No	Yes No	Yes No
8. Your company had a new recruit handbook which was kept up-to-date.	Yes No	Yes No	Yes No
9. Welcoming events were scheduled to help new recruits get acquainted.	Yes No	Yes No	Yes No
10. Publicity about the new recruit was circulated.	Yes No	Yes No	Yes No
11. New recruits had the opportunity to ask questions when they didn't understand something.	Yes No	Yes No	Yes No

Circle the number that best overall describes the orientation these new recruits received.

1	2	3	4	5
Poor	Needs Improvement	Not Sure	Good	The Best

Planning the Orientation Program

By failing to plan, you are planning to fail. This old adage relates to many business applications but holds especially true for the Orientation Program. This section will cover four key areas to ensure that your orientation program is successful. They are:

1. Reinforce the Opportunity Decision;

2. Make them feel welcome;

3. Commerce training; and

4. Commit to a 90 Day Plan.

Reinforce the Opportunity Decision

Orientation is a great way to allow the new recruit to confirm in their own mind that they have made a wise choice in applying and accepting a position in your organization. It is highly probable that your new recruit could have applied for other opportunities besides this one. To reduce the incidence of "Buyers Remorse" (the new recruits second-guessing their decision), the leader can use the orientation period to reinforce the opportunity decision.

Make Them Feel Welcome

How would you treat a client who was considering purchasing $15,000 of goods from your organization? Chances are you would treat them like royalty. New recruits are equally important. Set a positive first impression—roll out the red carpet. Here is a good question: why is it that most companies reward people that leave by giving "going away" parties and are neutral when new recruits come on board? Would it not be more beneficial to celebrate the arrival of new recruits? An easy way to provide such a welcome is to designate a room and time to invite team members to meet the new person and enjoy coffee and doughnuts.

Publicizing the hiring decision is another way to make the recruit feel welcome. There are two primary ways to publicize a hiring decision, internal and external. Internally, an announce-ment memo could be sent to all team members, or an article could be posted on the company website.

External publicity can be in the form of a press release with photo in the business section of the local newspaper or trade journals. It is important that the organization convey to the new recruit that they are pleased that they joined the organization. It is also a good idea to remind the new hire that help is available and any questions or concerns that he/she might have will be dealt with. Do everything in your power to ensure that the new person feels welcome.

Commence Training

Orientation provides an opportunity to start the new person on the right track. A well-planned orientation program will set the stage for all training and development that follows. During the orientation process the skills needed to perform the basic job can be taught. Without the benefit of a progressive orientation the recruit is left on their own to figure things out for themselves. This method is impersonal and time-consuming, as well as inefficient.

New recruits lacking essential information or receiving incorrect or misleading information can learn/develop bad habits. When the stage is set by giving proper direction, clear tasks and specific information, a new recruit will be more receptive to training and will make fewer costly errors.

Commit to a 90 Day Plan

Everyone should want the new recruit to succeed, therefore it's in the best interest of both parties for the leader to invest a bit of time to develop with the new recruit a 90 Day Plan for the first three months. Generally speaking people find it difficult to focus on key tasks and goals beyond 90 days, so why not plan the recruit's development and performance in a series of 90 day plans? As the first 90 day plan draws to an end, then both the leader and the recruit should discuss the performance of the first 90 days, set new learning, development and performance targets and incorporate those into the second 90 day plan.

One of the great benefits of having the leader coach the new recruit is that the leader can share their experience so that the recruit can quickly capitalize on the 80/20 principle. This principle, introduced in Chapter Five as it relates to self management, similarly recognizes that 20% of the tasks in any job contribute towards 80% of the success. Leaders that coach their new recruits as to which 20% of the position's tasks yield the 80% which will have provided a huge service to their people.

Several key factors that should be remembered when considering team development are modelling, learning and success. First, the leader should "model" self-development by constantly investing in their own personal/professional development. Second, the leader should also foster a "Learning Organization" atmosphere that highly encourages all team members to actively engage in their own training and development. Lastly, the leader should expect their people to be successful in their training and development efforts. The next chapter deals with one of the most important issues in retention...motivating the team.

Chapter SEVEN

Motivating Your Team

The best method of retaining great people is for the leader to create a positive team environment whereby people feel both happy and productive. The only way that this can be accomplished is when people are self-motivated. This chapter will focus on many elements surrounding motivation as well as dispelling several common myths on the subject.

The most powerful human motivators are recognition and rewards. Nothing propels people towards peak performance like having their efforts noticed, appreciated and rewarded. Wise leaders understand and accept that people have shortcomings. However, they choose to focus on their people's strengths. One example of this is attitude. If you consider the necessary elements required to be successful at any job, you will note that it takes a combination of skills, knowledge and attitude. Skills and knowledge together equals the person's ability to do the job. Just possessing the ability to do the job isn't enough to guarantee peak performance. One's attitude accounts for 85 per cent of one's success.

Attitude is closely linked to one's level of motivation. Now, a lot of leaders feel that it's their responsibility to motivate their teams. In fact, it's impossible to motivate another human being. However, the person can be enticed to make changes themselves. But when push comes to shove, the onus has to be on the individual to make the decision to change, and to motivate themselves.

Remember the example used in the Leadership chapter, "We can take a horse to water, but we can't make him drink?" In fact, we can walk the horse over to the water and say "Hey, horse, look outside, isn't that a hot day? Don't you feel hot? Aren't you thirsty? Look at that beautiful creek. Doesn't that water look great? Of course it does. Here, let me show you how good it is, and get down and actually drink the water.

Now even after doing all that, if the horse decides that he's not going to drink, he's not going to drink. There's nothing you can do to force him to drink. People are very similar. What you can do, as a leader, is to create an environment that makes it easier for your people to make the right decisions. In other words, to create a motivating environment. If you also have the expectation that it's up to you to change and motivate your staff, then you're going to set yourself up for some failure and some disappointments.

The diagram on the following page, "Motivation and Work Performance," is an attempt to explain what the average person requires in order to become self-motivated. I have looked at the work of two noted psychologists in the area, Maslow and Hertzberg. Both studied these issues quite extensively.

The following model represents my interpretation of Hertzberg and Maslow works combined. I then blended their work together and created this new model. Hertzberg and Maslow were saying essentially the same thing using different examples and different terms.

Motivation & Work Performance

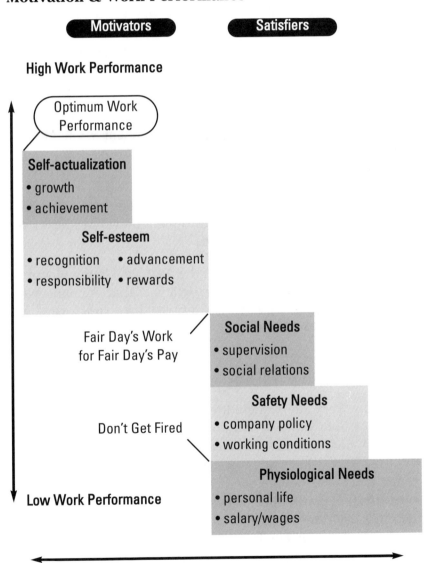

The model starts off at the bottom right "stepping stone" with very basic needs or **Physiological Needs**. Maslow called his theory "The Hierarchy of Needs." His premise was very simple: everyone starts out wanting and being motivated to acquire very basic or physiological needs. Some of these needs are personal safety, food, clothing, shelter.

Let's say you wanted somebody to dig a ditch, and the person you wanted to dig the ditch was very hungry and didn't have any food, then you came along and offered that person food (a basic need) to dig the ditch. That food becomes motivation for the individual. It will actually motivate them to want to do the work.

Now, assume you came across somebody else. But this other person was not very hungry. This person has their very basic needs fulfilled. Offering them more food will probably not motivate them. So they're not likely to dig the ditch for you, if that's the only incentive you can offer.

But Maslow said once we have our basic needs met, we're now triggered or motivated to move on to higher-level needs. So, the next level up is called **Safety Needs**.

Once this level has been met, then the next level in the hierarchy is called **Social Needs**. Maslow believed that humans were very social people, and would require love, nurturing and supportive relationships.

Once these three basic levels have been met, the next step in the Hierarchy of Needs is **Self-Esteem**.

Back to my very simple definition of self-esteem. It's how much you like or love yourself. I'm not talking about someone who's conceited, but someone who can simply look at him/herself and say, "Hey, sure I have some weaknesses, but I also have some strengths." These people can acknowledge their own good and be comfortable with themselves. And that's a very important measure. Any time you can offer somebody some way or some conditions that will satisfy his/her need for a high level of self-esteem, that becomes very motivational.

Lastly, Maslow said the highest level within the Hierarchy of Needs is something called **Self-Actualization**. Self-actualization is simply when you're walking down the road of life and you're totally satisfied and you have a (wonderful) balance in every area of your life. That's being totally self-actualized.

Now, Hertzberg viewed motivation in the individual as it related to the work he/she did. What he did was divide the model down the center. He broke it down into two sides. On one side, he had something called **Satisfiers**. And on the other side he had the **Motivators**.

Now another word for "Satisfiers" is "Hygiene Factors." Now why are they called "Hygiene Factors?" Well, looking back to when you were young in school, remember the public health nurse who made periodic visits? What did she normally say? She would say in order to maintain good personal hygiene, you have to brush your teeth, comb your hair, wash your face...so on and so forth. Let me ask you a question. If you brush your teeth on a regular basis three times a day, that's great. But if you start brushing your teeth maybe 20,30,40 times a day, will you become healthier? I would suggest that not only would you not become healthier, but you may even become ill by actually doing some damage to your gums. Now, on the flip side, if one day you just simply stop brushing your teeth, you also could become ill because of the onset of cavities and germs and so on and so forth. So why is it called "Hygiene Factors?" Basically, the whole idea is if you don't supply these core needs to the employee over the long haul, then the employee in a sense will become "sick." These needs are similar to Maslow's first three basic needs levels. One (Physiological), having adequate wage and salary, means having enough money to live and enough time away from the job to have some sort of decent personal life. Two (Safety), to have pro-active and safe working conditions, and to have a humane company policy. Three (Social), having the opportunity to interact with a supportive leader and positive team members.

These three areas put together, if given in abundance, don't actually make for a healthy person. Nor does it make a peak performer. However, according to Hertzberg, if we remove any one of these core elements over a long period of time, even the most satisfied, most highly motivated individuals will start to drop off. Their level of productivity and motivation will drop right down to the point where they're only going to give you enough performance so they don't get fired.

Now, if you provide your people with these three conditions and you only meet these three conditions, then what you can expect to get out of these people—at the very most—is only a fair day's work for a fair day's pay. If you're like me and you require absolute peak performers working for your organization, then you will have to "pay" a little bit more, and I'm not necessarily talking about salary.

What's the price you will have to pay for peak performers? Let's look at the other side of the diagram. You have to provide true motivators. You have to provide the pre-conditions within the work environment to excite your people so that they become self-motivated. What are these five motivators?

- A sense of *Responsibility*: People need to feel that their level of responsibility will actually grow over a period of time within the job.

- Rewards: Michael LeBoeuf, author of The Greatest Management Principle in the World, said "The things that get rewarded get done; the key is to reward the right behaviors." Some of the most powerful rewards are not based on money; they are simple, tangible everyday items that propel ordinary people to accomplish extraordinary results. The main point to remember is that, it's not so much the item that counts it's what the reward represents. I have seen rational adults scramble to earn a $ 10 T-shirt because that reward was physical proof that they accomplished a goal and they were publicly recognized as doing so. The best thing to do is to recognize and reward the top 20 % of your people in a high energy, entertaining public forum surrounded by their team mates. There are literally hundreds of ideas for rewards, the key is to have fun and be creative, feel free to ask your people for reward suggestions. The following is a small list of possible rewards:

- T-shirts/sweat shirts
- Ball caps
- Plaques/ trophies/medals
- Corporate rings/watches/ pens
- Certificates of Accomplishment
- Gift baskets
- Bottle of fine wine/Champagne
- Briefcase or portfolio with corporate name
- Gift certificate for a Restaurant or a store
- Trip for two
- Certificate for a day at the spa
- Personal Development Book/DVD
- Crystal/ figurines/sculptures
- Dinner for two
- Tickets to music concert or sporting event
- Motivational Prints

- *Advancement*: There has to exist an opportunity for advancement within the organization.

- *Recognition*: Everyone seeks feedback. One of the challenges, of course, is that sometimes the only feedback given from leaders is when something is wrong. One of the cautions I give my clients is not to get involved in what I call "Peek-a-boo management." This is when you hide around a corner and peer with one eye and wait until somebody messes up so you can say, "Peek-a-boo, gotcha. Now I'm going to get you."

There's a challenge with that sort of mindset. If an individual is doing something wrong, it must be corrected immediately, so it doesn't become a habit. However, looking at this from the opposite perspective, Ken Blanchard said it perfectly in his book *The One-Minute Manager.* "Catch them doing something right. Management should be deliberately catching staff doing something right." Not only saying, "Good job." But, "let me tell you specifically what you did right, what I liked about it, and the positive effect it has on the organization."

Now if you take the time to do this, the person will love the positive feedback. They're going to feel very good about the process. It's going to add to the rapport and the relationship between you and your team. And, perhaps even more importantly, they're going to continue the positive behavior.

- *Achievement:* Your people need the opportunity to achieve success in the workplace.

- An opportunity for *Personal Growth* can be achieved through promotions, more responsibilities and senior tasks, to name a few.

Before I go further in my discussion it would be appropriate to take the time to dispel 10 common Motivational Myths.

1. Cash Is King

    The idea that money is the only human motivator is perhaps the most common—and maybe even the most dangerous—of all the Motivational Myths. In fact, money is not a motivator in the long run. If someone doesn't have enough money to pay their bills and take care of their debts, then of course money becomes a motivator. This is a very primary need within the Hierarchy of Needs, according to Maslow.

    Once someone has enough money to meet their basic needs, and perhaps just a little bit left over, money becomes much less of a motivator. The nature of the job, the type of people, the work hours: all these things become much more important factors in motivating the person.

For example, have you ever known anyone—perhaps even yourself, who has been offered a different job that would have paid a lot more money than what he/she was making, but he/she decided not to take that job because of a number of other variables? Maybe it was the kind of work that led them to this choice, where they would have to be geographically, the hours, and so on and so forth. So here's proof that money is not the only human motivator

2. Motivation Equals Productivity

Although there is some sort of linkage between people that are highly motivated and those that are highly productive, there isn't a 100 percent cause—effect relationship. There could be someone who is highly motivated, really wants to do the job, is very enthusiastic, and has a wonderful attitude, but doesn't have the training. He/she doesn't have the background skills and knowledge, or the aptitude. For example, just because you want to be a brain surgeon, you really believe that you're a brain surgeon, and you've even visualized in your mind being a successful brain surgeon—if you haven't gone to medical school, and you haven't taken the time to study it and spend the years involved in preparing to become a brain surgeon, you will not have the abilities required to be a brain surgeon.

3. You Can Motivate Another Person

As you probably already know, nobody can make a smoker stop smoking, an alcoholic stop drinking, or a gambler stop gambling. No leader can cause an individual to be motivated. But a leader can provide the means and the atmosphere for people to motivate themselves.

A person will be motivated when he/she has an individual need that is currently un-met. When this need exists, the individual will naturally take steps to satisfy this need. As a leader, you must determine and present to your team a means or a strategy to satisfy this need while tying into the specific objectives of the organization, and then, monitor the results.

4. Happy People Are Productive People

    Happy people are definitely happy people. And that's nice. But that is not enough. That's not enough if you're looking for highly productive people. When push comes to shove in business, what you are really looking for is productivity and output. And someone smiling is not enough. The best scenario, of course, is to have a highly productive individual who also happens to be happy, enthusiastic and is a true team player.

5. What Motivates Me Motivates Everyone Else

    Unfortunately, motivators are not universal. One person may be absolutely delighted that you cared enough that you remembered their birthday. And in doing so, they may improve output by several hundred percent. Another person, however, may sneer when the same effort is shown to them, and may actually show no improvement in productivity. Some people simply want to do their job on a nine-to-five basis, they work at a fair, but even pace, they are neither satisfied nor dissatisfied, and they are not upwardly mobile. They do not want to take on any more responsibility.

    Other people need constant prodding, encouragement, and hand-holding. Their leaders are always trying to think of ways to provide incentives that boost their productivity.

    Then some people seem to be naturally self-motivated and are powerhouses of productivity.

    The point is that people are different. Therefore, you have to make sure that you tailor some of your activities to each person to try to meet their specific motivational requirements.

6. Punishment is the Best Form of Motivation

   If you can't get someone to do the job, you can always resort to some form of punishment, can't you? You can teach them a lesson. Well, maybe you can, and it might have a short-term benefit. But behavioral psychologists have demonstrated in various studies that over time negative reinforcement is less effective as a means of changing long-term behavior than positive reinforcement

   One of the cautions I would like to say at this point, though, is not to apply discipline in the hope that you can whip your employees into shape. It can be detrimental to the relationship, not to mention it can undermine the integrity of the individual, and at best, it's only a short-term fix.

7. The Leader Doesn't Have To Be Personally Motivated To Have A Motivated Team

   To this I say hogwash! It's absolutely imperative that the captain of the team—the leader—has to be motivated and has to encourage everyone to manage themselves. The best way to do this is through mirroring, by being the team's role model. To best accomplish this you, the leader should simply live the motivational life. Then people will look up to you and mirror what you do.

8. If My People Are Motivated, I'll Easily Be Able To See It

   This is a common misconception in many "management" circles. Unfortunately, motivation can't be measured by some sort of "smile-o-meter." Some people are naturally stoic. Their seemingly lacklustre demeanor is not necessarily a reflection of a lack of motivation on their part, it might just represent their personality. They don't show their enthusiasm very much. Yet when you look at the end result, they're highly productive people. They're very motivated to do what is necessary on their job.

9. It's Solely Up To The Leaders To Motivate The Team

That's simply not true. It's up to every single individual within the organization to motivate and to be self-motivated. But it has to start from somewhere. It has to start from the very top down, from the CEO of the organization. These individuals have to be motivated. They have to be able to exude a real energy and charisma about them. And they have to be able to sell their vision of the organization to everyone within the company.

10. If 75% of Your People are Motivated, That's Good Enough

Even if you have a very small percentage of your team who is unmotivated and has the wrong kind of attitude, this can ruin the corporate culture within your organization very quickly. All you need is one "bad apple" to spoil the whole "bushel." If just one person within your department or organization is de-motivated, that attitude can easily spread to other people on the team.

Here are some ideas on how to avoid this situation. 1) Try to intercede in any sort of negative discussions that take place by helping people turn the negatives into positives. 2) Make an extra effort to provide additional incentives to the entire team. 3) Hold frequent group meetings in which you can head off many of the negative vibes and actually deal with any real concerns that the unhappy person may be expressing.

How do you determine what your people really want? As I mentioned before, no two people are the same. Consequently, no single motivator is going to work as well with each and every one of your people.

To motivate effectively with non-monetary incentives, you need to know more about what the various motivators are. You need to know what will work with each and every one of your staff.

The reality is that the values of today are very different than the values of the workers of the 1950's and '60's. Because of high-tech information, the advances in media, and a myriad of other factors, today's workers are better educated, more independent, and less interested in following orders. They are more loyal to themselves than to the organization, and they are more concerned and vocal about meeting their own personal needs. The contemporary worker wants meaningful, challenging work. A lot more of his/her time is spent in leisure activities. He/she has a very strong need for feedback, recognition, rewards and would like to see immediate payback for the efforts put into a job.

What is the quickest way for you to determine what really motivates your people? First, ask them. Go to your people and ask them specifically what they like most and least about their jobs. Ask them questions such as "What are some of the things the company is doing that increases self-esteem? What are some of the things that the company does that decreases levels of self-esteem?" Their answers can be the starting point in discovering what motivates each and every member of your team.

The second thing you could do is to find out what your people do in their spare time, both at work and at home. This will tell you more about what's important to them.

Thirdly, look to previous experiences within the company. What sort of tasks or experiences has the person responded very favourably to in the past? What types of projects or assignments really created a high level of productivity? What types of assignments created apathy in the person?

Can we learn from this analysis? A more formalized method of determining what motivates your staff is to use a survey designed by Dick Berry. His survey is called the "Motiquiz III." This survey contains 45 statements describing different situations.

Motiquiz is an exercise to determine motivational needs. For each of the following statements check those that are most important in motivating you to do your best work. Select the ten most important statements. When you're done, then refer to the scoring guide at the bottom after you've made your selections.

629: Job security because of seniority or employment contract arrangements.

847: Being trusted to do my job the way I think it should be done.

333: Participating in a workgroup conversation.

311: Having adequate shelter to protect from the elements.

836: Having a job which allows me the time with my family.

151: Having an opportunity for personal growth.

937: Socializing with my friends.

743: Being considered for advancement opportunity.

431: Working with other people.

819: Having children.

458: Doing something meaningful with my life.

757: Being in a position to contribute new ideas.

828: Having an associate that looks out for my interests.

215: Not having to do exhausting work or do extra work at home.

421: Having steady work.

654: Being able to express my full potential.

327: Knowing that I will always have a job.

912: Having rest breaks with nourishments available.

924: Having a healthy working environment.

548: Being given a new interesting job.

256: Having the opportunity for self-improvement.

722: Having protection from physical harm.

352: Being able to learn and grow in my work.

735: Including other people in what I do.

949: Being selected for an exclusive award.

234: Being involved with work associates in social and recreational activities.

616: Being sexually satisfied.

146: Having a responsible person tell me when I've done a good job.

539: Having an active part in work-related social activities.

341: Knowing that other people respect me and my work.

132: Acceptance as a workgroup member.

225: Having insurance or other protective benefits.

444: Having others recognize the importance of my job.

853: Having a new and exciting job challenge.

113: Having enough food to eat each day.

245: Not having to be responsible to other people.

517: Having personal comfort in my working environment.

126: Knowing what is expected of me in my work.

559: Having the opportunity to express myself fully and creatively.

718: Having good air to breathe.

638: Working with persons I want to associate with.

642: Having a position of authority.

523: A guaranteed income.

955: The personal satisfaction of a job well done.

414: The assurance that I will have adequate clothing to protect myself from the elements.

Scoring Instructions for the Motiquiz

To determine the results, the statements are divided into five categories intended to represent the five levels in Maslow's Hierarchy of Needs. The second digit in each statement number indicates the category. These categories are (1) Physiological; (2) Safety and Security; (3) Social Needs; (4) Self-esteem; (5) Self-actualization.

The person's motivational needs are suggested by the numbers of selections in each category. For example, if the person had one in (1), two in (2), one in (3), four in (4), and two in (5), the percentage would be 10 percent Physiological, 20 percent Safety Needs, 10 percent Social Needs, 40 percent Self-esteem, and 20 percent for Self-actualization.

Another method of finding out what motivates each individual is to have them fill out the Values Preference Chart listed below.

Values Preference Chart

	Low				High
IDENTIFYING PERSONAL VALUES	1	2	3	4	5
Accomplishment					
Acknowledgement					
Challenge					
Cooperation					
Creativity					
Expertise					
Friendship					
Honesty					
Independence					
Instruction					
Intimacy					
Responsibility					
Organization					
Pleasure					
Quality					
Recognition					
Security					
Tranquility					
Empathy					
Variety					
Wealth					

Values Interpretation Chart

VALUE	PRIMARY NEED	RELATED FEAR
Accomplishment	Achievement	Failure
Acknowledgement	Appreciation	Being Unappreciated
Challenge	Stimulation	Stagnation
Cooperation	Unity	Dissension
Creativity	To Express Self	Repression
Expertise	To Feel Competent	Incompetent, Ordinary
Friendship	To Influence Others	Being Separated
Honesty	Trust	Deception
Independence	Be In Self Control	Being Controlled
Instruction	Understanding	Confusion
Intimacy	Close To Another	Emotionally Alone
Organization	Order	Chaos
Pleasure	Play, Entertainment	Boredom
Quality	High Standards	Low Standards
Recognition	Attention	Being Ignored
Responsibility	In Control	Not In Control
Security	Peace Of Mind	Being In Debt
Tranquility	Harmony	Conflict
Empathy	Feelings Understood	Feelings Ignored
Variety	Experience	Routine
Wealth	Rewards	Poverty

Developed by C.R.G Ltd.

In short, I am saying that when it comes to human motivation, cash is definitely not king. Money is at best only a short term answer to dealing with challenges of poor morale, low productivity, or high absenteeism. Today's workers require more: a real commitment and a sense of loyalty from the organization. They want and need to be involved in the decision-making process.

They need an opportunity for advancement, personal growth, and challenge. They require all the things covered in this chapter, and they need them on a consistent basis. If you're not prepared to fulfill these requirements regularly, after a while what you're going to have is a "sick" performer.

And a sick performer can easily be seen. It's one who is demotivated, dissatisfied with the position and disenchanted. The net result is low productivity and high turnover. You know the phenomenal cost of hiring and training great people. So the key is to pay a little bit now. If you're not prepared to pay a little now to keep your great people, then it's going to cost you a whole lot more in the end.

Conclusion

Now that you have read this book, keep referring to it as a constant source of practical information to ensure that you recruit & retain great people. Remember that a great person is someone that is:

- Goal oriented with a burning desire to win.
- Reputable with high moral standards and integrity.
- Enthusiastic about self-development.
- Attitude of positive professionalism.
- Tenacious, they "do it" until the job gets done.

Once you apply the principles covered within this book, the odds of being successful are in your favor.

Best of Success!

Dr. Denis L. Cauvier

If you enjoyed *Attracting, Selecting & Retaining Great People* you may be interested in the international best-selling book *The ABCs of Making Money* written by Dr. Denis L. Cauvier and Alan Lysaght. Readers of the book can obtain a **complementary, confidential, no obligation** Financial Makeover! For more information send an email to: info@abcsofmakingmoney.com

To order The ABCs of Making Money please visit:

www.abcsofmakingmoney.com

To order more copies of this book please contact:

dcauvier@magi.com • 613.623.5656

Dr. Denis L. Cauvier Seminars International is committed to providing its clients with customized solutions tailored to their unique requirements. Practical, results-oriented training, consulting and professional speaking based solutions are available in the following areas:

Team Development

- How to Attract & Select Great People
- How to Keep Your People Productive & Happy
- How to Reduce Team Turnover

Sales/ Customer Service Development

- Sales Mastery
- Low Cost, High Impact Strategic Selling
- Turning the One-time Buyer Into a Lifelong Customer
- Achieving Sales Results by Propelling Your Team Into Action

Wealth Development

- The ABCs of Making Money
- The ABCs of Building a Powerful Legacy
- The ABCs of Business Success

Personal Development

- Achieve It! A Personal Journey
- The Art & Science of Stress Management

For more information regarding how Dr. Denis L. Cauvier Seminars International services can assist your organization, please contact:

dcauvier@magi.com • 613.623.5656